SPOTLIGHT

MICHIGAN'S TRAVERSE BAYS & MACKINAC ISLAND

LAURA MARTONE

Contents

Traverse City and Northwest Michigan 4

Planning Your Time 7
History 7

Traverse City and Vicinity ...8

Sights..............................9
Festivals 12
Shopping...........................13
Sports and Recreation 14
Accommodations 17
Food...............................18
Information and Services............19
Getting There and Around 19
Interlochen Center for the Arts 20
Interlochen State Park 20
Benzie County......................20

The Leelanau Peninsula 21

Sleeping Bear Dunes
    National Lakeshore................21
Leland to Northport................27
Leelanau State Park 28
Suttons Bay.......................28
Wineries of Grand Traverse Bay 29
Events 30
Diving.............................30
Accommodations and Food 31
Information and Services............31
Getting There and Around 31

Manistee to Cadillac.........32

Manistee..........................32
Ludington 33

Pentwater and Silver Lake...........34
Manistee National Forest 34
Cadillac 36
Golf...............................36
Accommodations 36
Food...............................37
Information and Services............37
Getting There and Around 37

Charlevoix and Vicinity.....38

Sights..............................38
Charlevoix Venetian Festival.........40
Shopping..........................40
Recreation 41
Accommodations and Food 41
Information and Services............41
Getting There and Around 42
Fisherman's Island State Park 43
Lake Charlevoix....................43
Ellsworth and Vicinity..............45
Beaver Island......................46

Petoskey and Vicinity 48

Sights..............................49
Entertainment......................51
Shopping..........................51
Sports and Recreation 52
Accommodations and Food 53
Information and Services............54
Getting There and Around 54
Little Traverse Bay..................54
Lake Michigan Shore 55

Mackinac Island and Northeast Michigan 59

Planning Your Time 62
History 62

Mackinaw City 63
Sights............................ 63
Shopping.......................... 66
Accommodations and Food 66
Information and Services........... 67
Getting There and Around 67

Mackinac Island 68
Sights............................ 68
Shopping...........................73
Recreation 73
Accommodations 73
Food..............................74
Information and Services........... 75
Getting There and Around 75

Cheboygan and Vicinity 77
Sights.............................77
Recreation 77
Accommodations and Food 78
Information and Services........... 78
Getting There and Around 78
The Inland Waterway............... 79

Rogers City to Alpena 80
Sights............................ 80
Diving in Thunder Bay.............. 83
Accommodations and Food 83

Information and Services........... 84
Getting There and Around 84
Presque Isle...................... 85

Oscoda to West Branch..... 86
Sights............................ 86
Shopping.......................... 87
Canoeing on the Au Sable River 88
Accommodations and Food 88
Information and Services........... 89
Getting There and Around 89
Huron National Forest.............. 89
Houghton and Higgins Lakes........ 93

Grayling Area 94
Recreation 94
Accommodations and Food 96
Information and Services........... 97
Getting There and Around 97
George Mason River Retreat Area.... 98
Hartwick Pines State Park.......... 98

Gaylord Area 99
Sights............................ 99
Alpenfest 99
Sports and Recreation 101
Accommodations and Food 102
Information and Services...........103
Getting There and Around 103
Pigeon River Country State Forest ...104

TRAVERSE CITY AND NORTHWEST MICHIGAN

Although the entire state is defined by water, perhaps no region is more dramatically contoured by lakes, bays, and rivers than the northwestern corner of Michigan's Lower Peninsula, especially the coast surrounding Traverse City, the area's largest town and the self-proclaimed "Cherry Capital of the World." The aquamarine waters of Lake Michigan mingle with two stunning coastal bays: Grand Traverse Bay, a majestic, 32-mile-long inlet partially bisected by the slender Old Mission Peninsula, and Little Traverse Bay, situated farther north near Petoskey, a town famous for its high concentration of Petoskey stones, the fossilized coral rock that was named Michigan's state stone in 1965.

On summer weekends, the lakeside towns of Traverse City, Charlevoix, and Petoskey seem to grow exponentially. While some fear the overdevelopment that's encroached upon this area in recent years, visitors continue to flock to the coast, embracing a wide array of diversions, including windsurfing, fishing charters, bike trails, chic restaurants and galleries, golf and ski resorts, and old-fashioned downtown shopping districts. Along the coast, visitors can also admire a number of historic lighthouses, from the 1858 Beaver Head Lighthouse on Beaver Island to the picture-perfect 1870 Mission Point Lighthouse amid Grand Traverse Bay. Beyond the many islands and breezy shores of Lake Michigan, numerous inland lakes pepper this diverse region.

Outdoor enthusiasts embrace the pristine beaches and clear waters of Northwest Michigan, a breathtaking area that's also home to many state parks, several state forests,

HIGHLIGHTS

LOOK FOR ◖ TO FIND RECOMMENDED SIGHTS, ACTIVITIES, DINING, AND LODGING.

◖ **National Cherry Festival:** This annual celebration of Michigan's booming cherry industry attracts over 500,000 participants every July. Activities include cherry pie-eating and pit-spitting contests, a grand buffet, a golf tournament, and a cherry-related farmers market (page 12).

◖ **Traverse City Film Festival:** Since 2005, Michigan's premier film festival – cofounded by filmmaker Michael Moore – has lured thousands of filmmakers and cinema lovers to Traverse City for a week of eclectic screenings, panel discussions, parties, and musical performances (page 13).

◖ **Interlochen Center for the Arts:** Interlochen has, for more than 85 years, cultivated a passion for the arts. Besides offering a summer camp for young artists and year-round programs for adults, this renowned institute invites visitors to attend dance performances, film screenings, art exhibitions, and more (page 20).

◖ **Sleeping Bear Dunes National Lakeshore:** This one-of-a-kind national park features some of the largest freshwater dunes in the world, not to mention two isolated islands in Lake Michigan. Climb the dunes, explore historic buildings, and pursue a wide array of outdoor activities, from hiking to kayaking to scuba diving (page 21).

◖ **Wineries of Grand Traverse Bay:** Wineries and tasting rooms pepper the Leelanau and Old Mission Peninsulas, the destinations of choice for countless connoisseurs (page 29).

◖ **Loda Lake National Wildflower Sanctuary:** Nestled within the Manistee National Forest, north of White Cloud, this is the only wildflower sanctuary ever established in a U.S. national forest. Stroll through oak-maple woodlands, old pine plantations, and a shrub swamp boasting a slew of plant species (page 35).

and the expansive Manistee National Forest. Located along the western edge of the Leelanau Peninsula—known for its scenic, award-winning wineries—lies another natural wonder, Sleeping Bear Dunes National Lakeshore, one of the Midwest's finest natural escapes and a popular destination for anglers, hikers, bikers, skiers, kayakers, and amateur geologists. While there's plenty to keep anyone occupied, the most eye-catching features are the pyramidal dunes themselves, some of which rise over 400 feet high, constituting the largest freshwater dunes in the world and offering an unparalleled view of Glen Lake and the surrounding hills.

TRAVERSE CITY AND NORTHWEST MICHIGAN

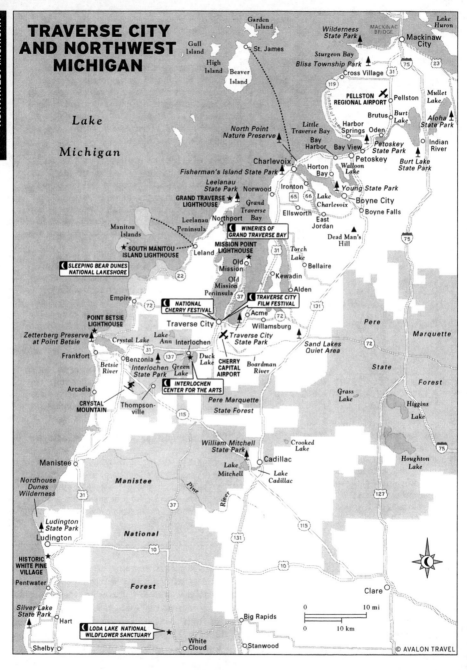

© TRAVERSE CITY TOURISM

hiking near the South Manitou Island Lighthouse

PLANNING YOUR TIME

Extending from the southern edge of Manistee National Forest to the Mackinac Bridge, Northwest Michigan is indeed a sprawling region. Although you can reach the area via boat, bus, or plane, you'll find it easier to navigate with a vehicle—whether your own or a rented one. By car, you can get here via US-31 from Muskegon, US-131 from Grand Rapids, US-10 from Midland, and I-75 from the Upper Peninsula.

If your schedule's tight, plan a weekend getaway to Traverse City. Two weeks, however, will ensure time to experience more than just the Cherry Capital, including Sleeping Bear Dunes, the Leelanau Peninsula, Manistee National Forest, Beaver Island, and several coastal towns, beaches, and golf resorts.

Summer is exceedingly popular in Northwest Michigan, especially in the resort towns and during the area's annual festivals. So, if you aren't a fan of crowds, try to come in spring, fall, or winter. After all, even during the off-season, the region will appeal to art lovers, golfing enthusiasts, beachcombers, wine connoisseurs, cross-country skiers, and many other fun-seekers.

For more details about Northwest Michigan, contact the **West Michigan Tourist Association** (WMTA, 741 Kenmoor Ave., Ste. E, Grand Rapids, 616/245-2217, www.wmta. org).

HISTORY

Traverse City has been hosting visitors ever since the French explorers and fur traders passed through the area in the 1600s, soon spreading word of the treacherous canoe passage across the gaping mouth of the bay, *la grande traversée.* Since then, the Traverse region has attracted everyone from James Jesse Strang, a self-proclaimed king who set his sights on ruling Beaver Island, to a family called the Hemingways, who summered for decades on the shores of Walloon Lake.

But it was the Victorian "resorters" who left an indelible mark. Summer visitors began trickling in around the 1860s, escaping hot and sticky Midwestern cities for the lake's crisp breezes and gentle shores. Soon, they were flooding into communities like Charlevoix and Petoskey, by steamship and by train. The "old money" of Chicago, Detroit, and Cleveland built exclusive summer homes. The simply rich stayed in grand pastel-painted hotels. Good Christians came to the church-run camps, which soon evolved from canvas tents to frilly Victorian cottages that remain well preserved today. Decade after decade, they attended Sousa concerts in the park, sailed dinghies across the harbor, and sipped lemonade on verandas overlooking the beautiful blue-green bays.

Today, the two bays, Grand Traverse Bay and Little Traverse Bay, anchor one of the state's most popular vacation areas, where the air is still crisp and clean, and the waters are still clear and accessible. Like elsewhere, development is a hot-button issue, as slick developments for urban visitors push aside the quaint cottages and small-town life that made everyone want to visit here in the first place. The populations of lakeside Traverse City, Charlevoix, and Petoskey can grow several-fold on a good July weekend. Legions of "designer" golf resorts, blue-ribbon fly-fishing rivers, back-road biking routes, and some of the Midwest's largest ski resorts have drawn visitors inland, too.

But for all this activity, the region's past still weaves into the scene—the lyrical French names, the proud old lighthouses, the industrialists' homes, the century-old family farms. Like the great dunes that ignore park boundaries and drift across the newly paved park roads, past and present jumble together here, some parts planned, other parts as wild as the wind.

Nowhere does that seem more apparent than on Beaver Island. Irish immigrants arrived here in the 1840s, fleeing the potato famine and looking for new opportunities. They built Beaver Island into one of the premier commercial fisheries on the Great Lakes, ringing the hooked harbor at St. James with docks, net sheds, and icehouses. At about the same time, a man named Jesse Strang arrived. A New Yorker who challenged Brigham Young and claimed to be the leader of the Mormons, he brought his faithful to Beaver Island, where he proclaimed himself king, took five wives,

began a newspaper, pushed the Irish off their land, and eventually was assassinated by two of his followers.

The Irish reclaimed their island, the population soared to nearly 2,000 by the turn of the 20th century, and today, more than a third of the island's 660 year-round residents are descendants of the original Irish immigrant families. It's no wonder, then, that St. Patrick's Day is one of the island's most celebrated holidays.

The parasitic lamprey eel and overfishing pretty much ruined the commercial fishing trade, and the island's other main industry, logging, disappeared when ships converted from wood-burning engines to fossil fuels. Today, residents earn their living coaxing a few crops out of the rocky, sandy soil or, more commonly, by running service businesses that make a lion's share of their annual wages in July and August. By and large, residents encourage the summer tourist trade and the business visitors bring to the island. There's more of a battle regarding those who build summer cottages. While the building trades are a mainstay of the island economy and many welcome the jobs new construction provides, plenty of others oppose development. It's the universal controversy, though, fought in rural areas all over the continent.

Traverse City and Vicinity

Traverse City sits at the foot of Grand Traverse Bay, a body of water with incredible color and clarity. From blue to green to aquamarine, it shifts hues like a chameleon warming in the sun. The bay, not surprisingly, remains the top vacation draw in Traverse City. In summer months, this water lover's playground hums with activity—filled with kayaks, fishing boats, Jet Skis, sailboards, cruising sailboats, and twin-masted tall ships—and the sand beaches fill up with sunbathers and volleyball players.

Though its population swells from 14,900 to nearly 300,000 in summer

months—especially during the National Cherry Festival—Traverse City has managed to accomplish what few "vacation towns" have: It remains a real community, where services like hardware stores and quick-print shops still operate alongside the gift shops and galleries. Locals actually use their pretty downtown area, and peaceful neighborhoods still thrive just a few blocks away. Traverse City has style *and* substance. Oh, there's no doubt tourism drives the economy here, but Traverse City's strong sense of place makes it all the more appealing to residents and visitors alike.

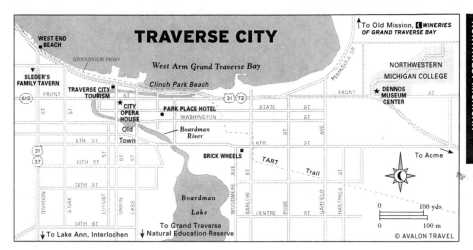

SIGHTS
Historic Sites and Museums

Downtown Traverse City abounds in Victorian architecture and historic buildings. One must-see is the 1892 red-brick **City Opera House** (106 E. Front St., 231/941-8082, www.city-operahouse.org), which is currently being restored to its Victorian splendor. Visitors can better appreciate the lovely theater by attending one of its regularly scheduled concerts, comedy shows, and other events.

On the campus of Northwestern Michigan College, the **Dennos Museum Center** (1701 E. Front St., 231/995-1055, www.dennosmuseum.org, 10am-5pm Mon.-Sat., 1pm-5pm Sun., $6 adults, $4 children) is a wonderful find. It houses one of the nation's finest collections of Inuit art, along with interactive exhibits in the Discovery Gallery that combine art, science, and technology.

In nearby Acme, the **Music House Museum** (7377 US-31 N, 231/938-9300, www.musichouse.org, 10am-4pm Mon.-Sat., noon-4pm Sun. May-Oct., 10am-4pm Fri.-Sat., noon-4pm Sun. Nov.-Dec., $10 adults, $3 children 6-15) is another surprise, showcasing a vast array of rare antique musical instruments, from 1870 to 1930. Its collection includes music boxes, jukeboxes, nickelodeons, pipe organs, and a hand-carved Belgian dance organ.

Old Mission Peninsula

The Old Mission Peninsula pierces north from Traverse City, a narrow sliver of land that neatly divides Grand Traverse Bay in two. This whaleback ridge stretches 22 miles, a quiet agrarian landscape cross-hatched with cherry orchards and vineyards. Nowhere else on earth grows more cherries per acre than the Old Mission Peninsula, where the surrounding waters, insulating snows, and cool summer air form the perfect microclimate for raising fruit. Veer off M-37 onto almost any country road to wander past the pretty, peaceful orchards.

Grapes also thrive on the Old Mission Peninsula, creating a burgeoning winemaking industry (www.wineriesofoldmission.com). (Though locals like to tell you it's because the peninsula sits at the same latitude as Bordeaux, France, they really should thank the moderating effects of the lake.) Most of the eight wineries here offer tours and tastings, and visiting them brings an extra benefit: The ridgetop roads of the Old Mission Peninsula come with incredible views that often take in both arms of Grand Traverse Bay.

Chateau Grand Traverse (12239 Center Rd., 231/223-7355 or 800/283-0247, www.cgtwines.com, 10am-7pm Mon.-Sat., 10am-6pm Sun. Memorial Day-Labor Day, 10am-6pm Mon.-Sat., 10am-5pm Sun. early Sept.-Oct.,

NORTHWEST MICHIGAN

© TRAVERSE CITY TOURISM

the City Opera House

10am-5pm daily Nov.-May), located nine miles north of Traverse City on M-37, was a pioneer in bringing European vinifera wines to the Midwest. It has a beautiful tasting room, with wonderful bay views, for tasting its internationally award-winning rieslings and ice wines. In addition, the winery offers tours as well as luxurious accommodations in its hilltop inn.

Just east of Bowers Harbor, **Bowers Harbor Vineyards** (2896 Bowers Harbor Rd., 231/223-7615 or 800/616-7615, www.bowersharbor.com, 10:30am-6pm Mon.-Sat., noon-6pm Sun. May-Oct., 10:30am-5pm Mon.-Sat., noon-5pm Sun. Nov.-Apr.) is a small, friendly, family-run winery, with a year-round tasting room.

Chateau Chantal (15900 Rue de Vin, 231/223-4110 or 800/969-4009, www.chateauchantal.com, 11am-8pm Mon.-Sat., 11am-6pm Sun. Memorial Day-Labor Day, 11am-7pm Mon.-Sat., 11am-6pm Sun. early Sept.-Oct., 11am-5pm daily Nov.-June) includes both a tasting room and a B&B in a

French chateau-inspired winery high on a hill. Winery tours are offered during the summer months; inexpensive wine-tastings are available all year. **Peninsula Cellars** (11480 Center Rd., 231/933-9787, www.peninsulacellars. com, 10am-6pm Mon.-Sat., noon-6pm Sun.) is one of the peninsula's newer wineries, with a tasting room in a converted 1896 schoolhouse.

The peninsula was named for the mission first built near its tip in 1829 by a Presbyterian minister who came from Mackinac to convert the Ojibwa and Ottawa. The **Mission Church** on M-37 in Old Mission is a replica, but it houses the original bell. A few displays tell the peninsula's early history and evolution into a fruit-growing region. Nearby, the 1842 **Dougherty House,** the region's first frame building, is the real thing. Once home to Reverend Peter Dougherty and his family, the homestead is currently undergoing restoration, after which the house and surrounding acreage will be open to the public. For more information about the Dougherty Homestead, consult the **Old Mission Peninsula Historical Society**

© LAURA MARTONE

the stunning view from Chateau Chantal

(www.omphistoricalsociety.org). In the meantime, you can stop by the **Old Mission General Store** (18250 Mission Rd., 231/223-4310), a 19th-century trading post filled with all manner of candy, wine, deli meats, and other supplies. After gathering your provisions, head east around Old Mission Harbor to **Haserot Beach,** a lovely curve of sand near the small protected harbor, ideal for a beachside picnic.

The **Mission Point Lighthouse** stands sentinel over the point, a pretty structure dating to 1870, along with its white clapboard keeper's home (now privately owned). The state has acquired several hundred acres around the lighthouse, including much of the rocky beach, land set aside for a possible future state park.

Beaches and Tours

The Old Mission Peninsula divides Grand Traverse Bay into two "arms." The West Arm (or West Bay) is the larger and deeper of the two, home to marinas, the bay's tall ship cruises, and a few commercial enterprises. The East Arm (or East Bay) is shallower, warmer, and ringed with sugary sand at its south end— prompting lodging and water-sports ventures along its shores.

Along with all the wonderful beaches on the Leelanau Peninsula, Traverse City has several right downtown. Most popular is **Clinch Park Beach** on West Bay, east of Union Street. A little farther west, at the foot of Division, **West End Beach** is the place to head for volleyball. On East Bay, **Bayside Park** has 600 feet of sand beach and a bathhouse, just off US-31 near the Acme turnoff.

The *Nauti-Cat* (231/947-1730, www. nauti-cat.com) offers varied cruises on West Bay aboard a 47-foot catamaran. The open-deck arrangement allows for up to 43 guests. Prices range from $15 for a 90-minute kids' cruise to $35 for a champagne sunset cruise. Reservations are recommended, but walk-ons are accepted if there's space. An authentic replica of an 18th-century wooden schooner, the *Tall Ship Manitou* (Dockside Plaza, 13390 S. West Bay Shore Dr., 231/941-2000,

© DANIEL MARTONE

sailing on the *Tall Ship Manitou*

www.tallshipsailing.com, $34-42 adults, $18-26 children) sets sail three times daily in July and August, cruising West Bay.

FESTIVALS

❰ National Cherry Festival

Without question, Traverse City's largest event is the **National Cherry Festival** (800/968-3380, www.cherryfestival.org, prices vary), which takes place every July in various locations throughout downtown Traverse City. First held in 1925, this annual celebration of Michigan's cherry industry attracts over 500,000 participants, who come for the parades and fireworks, live entertainment, turtle races, cherry pie-eating contests, a grand cherry-themed buffet, and a cherry farmers market. Participants will be able to taste a wide array of cherry-enhanced

TRAVERSE CITY ALE TRAIL

Traverse City has become quite a beer lov-. er's oasis. Even the Travel Channel has taken note, recently including Traverse City on its list of the "top seven beer destinations." *DRAFT Magazine*, meanwhile, named it one of three "emerging beer towns" in 2012. To celebrate the city's booming craft beer scene, the powers-that-be have created the **Traverse City Ale Trail** (www.tcaletrail. com), also known as the TC Ale Trail, a fun way to experience eight different microbreweries in the Traverse City area. To do so, you simply need to pick up a free TC Ale Trail passport at any of the participating breweries, most hotels and restaurants, or the Traverse City Visitors Bureau on West Grandview Parkway. Then, as you visit each of the featured breweries, just collect a unique stamp with any purchase. When you've visited all eight, return your completed passport to **The Filling Station Microbrewery** for a free, commemorative silicone pint glass. For an extra-credit prize, be sure to make a pit stop at the **Grand Traverse Distillery** (781 Industrial Cir., Ste. 5, 231/947-8635, www. grandtraversedistillery.com, 11:30am-5:30pm Mon.-Sat., noon-4pm Sun.), Michigan's oldest and largest vodka and whiskey distillery. Just remember that, given the spread-out nature of these breweries, you'll probably need to access them via vehicle, so be sure to drink and drive responsibly.

Here are the eight breweries that you'll encounter along the TC Ale Trail:

· **Beggars Brewery** (4177 Village Park Dr., Ste. C, www.beggarsbrewery.com): Established in 2011, this small production brewery and tap room is one of the newest to join the ranks of Traverse City's craft beer scene. As of late 2013, though, it had yet to open, so until it does, its stamp won't be required to complete your passport.

· **Brewery Ferment** (511 S. Union St., 231/735-8113, www.breweryferment.com, 3pm-10pm Mon.-Thurs., 3pm-midnight Fri., noon-midnight Sat.): Housed within a century-old building, this casual neighborhood spot offers a handful of flagship and specialty taps, such as the Old Town Brown, plus tasty bar snacks.

· **The Filling Station Microbrewery** (642 Railroad Pl., 231/946-8168, http://thefillingstationmicrobrewery.com, 11:30am-11pm Mon.-Thurs., 11:30am-midnight Fri.-Sat., noon-10pm Sun.): Situated in the city's historic railroad district, this casual pub provides handcrafted ales, wood-fired cuisine and cherry wines, produced by local wineries.

One of the busiest days, but well worth the fuss, is the first Sunday of the festival, when an air show features the astonishing flying skills of the U.S. Navy Blue Angels. Get there early, and plan to be camped out in the same spot for much of the day. If you're feeling really lucky, try entering the cherry pit-spitting contest, always a crowd pleaser.

◖ Traverse City Film Festival

The state's premier film event, the **Traverse City Film Festival** (various venues, 231/392-1134, www.traversecityfilmfest.org, tickets $10-75 pp), brings a bit of Hollywood to northern Michigan. Cofounded in 2005 by Academy Award-winning filmmaker Michael Moore, the festival lures more and more celebrities, filmmakers, and cinema buffs every summer (usually at the end of July or beginning of August). For an entire week, the festival showcases eclectic film screenings, informative panel discussions, various parties, and live musical performances; it also offers a terrific opportunity to see a few of your favorite movie stars in person.

SHOPPING

Traverse City's main east-west avenue, **Front Street,** is lined with dozens of cafés, galleries, and shops, offering everything from nautical home furnishings to cherry pies. Cobblestone **Union Street** marks Old Town, a growing area of arts and antiques.

If you have a desire for local produce and flatbreads, fresh salads, and pleasant views of adjacent Boardman Lake.

- **Jolly Pumpkin** (13512 Peninsula Dr., 231/223-4333, www.jollypumpkin.com, 11:30am-9pm Sun.-Thurs., 11:30am-10pm Fri.-Sat.): Located in a cottage-like setting on the Old Mission Peninsula, this popular restaurant, microbrewery, and distillery serves local artisan fare as well as spirits distilled on-site, wines from area vineyards, and craft beers.

- **Mackinaw Brewing Company** (161 E. Front St., 231/933-1100, www.mackinaw-brewing.com, 11am-10pm Mon.-Thurs., 11am-11pm Fri.-Sat., noon-10pm Sun.): Founded in 1997 and housed within the historic Beale Building, MBC was actually the first brewpub to open in downtown Traverse City. Besides offering wine, spirits, and a full menu of salads, sandwiches, steaks, fish, and smoked meats, it features house-brewed beers, such as the Peninsula Pale Ale and Harvest Moon Oatmeal Stout.

- **North Peak Brewing Company** (400 W. Front St., 231/941-7325, www.northpeak.net, 11am-11pm Mon.-Thurs., 11am-midnight Fri.-Sat., noon-10pm Sun.): Established in 1995, North Peak prepares handcrafted beers,

from the Mission Point Porter to Shirley's Irish Stout, in an on-site brewery. It also offers a full menu of soups, salads, sandwiches, hearth-baked pizzas, steaks, ribs, pasta dishes, and well-prepared local fish.

- **Right Brain Brewery** (225 E. 16th St., 231/944-1239, www.rightbrainbrewery.com, noon-11pm Mon.-Thurs., 11am-midnight Fri.-Sat., noon-9pm Sun.): Recently named one of the "top five local breweries in the nation," Right Brain definitely has an unpretentious atmosphere. This popular brewery is known for making award-winning, culinary-inspired beers, such as the creamy Smooth Operator and the CEO Stout, not to mention rotating signature, Belgian, and premium taps. While here, you can also sample hefty waffle sandwiches.

- **The Workshop Brewing Company** (221 Garland St., Ste. A, 231/421-8977, www.traversecityworkshop.com, 11am-10pm Mon.-Thurs., 11am-midnight Fri.-Sat., 11am-10pm Sun.): Relatively new to Traverse City, this innovative, ecofriendly brewery offers a welcoming atmosphere, a wide array of traditional, seasonal, and oak-aged beers, and several tasty, one-hander sandwiches that complement the beers.

canine jumping competition at the National Cherry Festival

other goodies, from soaps to soup mixes, browse the **Traverse City Sara Hardy Farmers Market** (www.traversecityfarmersmarket.com, 8am-noon Sat. May, 8am-noon Sat. and Wed. June-Oct.), along the banks of the Boardman River, between Union and Cass Streets.. Depending on the season, you'll find all manner of veggies, fruits, and flowers—and you can always count on the reliable muffin crop.

SPORTS AND RECREATION
Golf
Award-winning golf courses abound in the Traverse region, just a few minutes away from Traverse City. About three miles from town, **Elmbrook Golf Course** (1750 Townline Rd., 231/946-9180, www.elmbrookgolf.com, daily Apr.-Oct., $32 pp w/cart) is an older, unpretentious course, with lots of hills, valleys, and views of Grand Traverse Bay.

In Acme, about five miles east of Traverse City on US-31, you'll find one of the state's finest golfing destinations. The 900-acre **Grand Traverse Resort and Spa** (100 Grand Traverse Village Blvd., 231/534-6000, www.grandtraverseresort.com, daily Apr.-Oct., $35-140 pp) features two signature

courses: The Bear, a famously humbling course designed by Jack Nicklaus, with minute greens and deep, deep bunkers, and the Gary Player-designed Wolverine, a watery course with views of Grand Traverse Bay. Both tend to overshadow Spruce Run, the resort's other fine championship course, which, though less challenging, is equally stunning. Set amid an evergreen forest, Spruce Run can even be appreciated by bird-watchers; ducks, swans, and blue herons abound here. In addition to the courses, the resort provides comfortable accommodations, decent dining, a top-notch spa, an indoor water park, and a 24-hour dog care facility.

East of Acme, the rolling pine forests and old orchards of **High Pointe Golf Club** (5555 Arnold Rd., Williamsburg, 231/267-9900, daily Apr.-Oct., $30-79 pp w/cart) once earned it a spot among *Golf Magazine*'s 100 favorites. Meanwhile, the views of picturesque Torch Lake add an extra challenge to keeping your head down at the **A-Ga-Ming Golf Resort** (627 A-Ga-Ming Dr., Kewadin, 231/264-5081, www.a-ga-ming.com, daily Apr.-Oct., $20-84 pp), which is situated north of Acme via US-31 and offers two 18-hole courses: Torch and the relatively new Sundance.

MICHAEL MOORE'S SALUTE TO FILM

Perhaps Michigan's most infamous son, Michael Francis Moore was born in Flint in 1954. Years after studying journalism at the University of Michigan-Flint, Moore turned to filmmaking. His first film, *Roger & Me* (1989), was lauded by some as a biting indictment of the automotive industry, and has been considered by others as the start of Moore's truth-bending, politically charged style of filmmaking. In equal measure, he's been called a documentary filmmaker and a propaganda artist. Some of his rather slanted films include *The Big One* (1997), another exposé about greedy executives and callous politicians; the Oscar-winning *Bowling for Columbine* (2002), an exploration of America's violent culture; *Fahrenheit 9/11* (2004), Moore's take on how the Bush administration used the tragic 9/11 events to push its war agenda; *Sicko* (2007), a comparison of America's healthcare industry to others around the world; and *Capitalism: A Love Story* (2009), an indictment of corporate interests and how their dogged pursuit of high profits has negatively impacted the rest of society.

No matter what you might think of Moore's controversial films, his contribution to Michigan's modern culture is undeniable. In 2005, Moore – along with photographer John Robert Williams and author Doug Stanton – established the **Traverse City Film Festival (TCFF)**, a charitable, educational organization whose stated purpose is to preserve one of America's few native art forms: cinema. The festival, which owns and operates a year-round arthouse movie theater in the Cherry Capital (a theater that was generously donated to TCFF in 2007 by the Rotary Charities of Traverse City), also lures filmmakers and cinema buffs from around the world to its annual film festival, which usually occurs in late July or early August. This event, which has quickly become one of northern Michigan's biggest attractions, features panel discussions about the film industry in addition to screenings that include foreign flicks, American independent films, documentaries, and classic movies. Just be advised that, unlike most film festivals in the United States, TCFF doesn't accept submissions, which means that the films are often handpicked with a purpose, sometimes to serve Moore's extremely liberal agenda. For more information about the Traverse City Film Festival, visit www.traversecityfilmfest.org or call 231/392-1134.

Perhaps you'll find it surprising that the quiet countryside southwest of Traverse City is home to one of the best public golf courses in the state, but it's indeed true. Situated alongside a gorgeous stretch of Lake Michigan shoreline and accessible via M-22, the 18-hole **Arcadia Bluffs Golf Club** (14710 Northwood Hwy., Arcadia, 231/889-3001, www.arcadiabluffs.com, daily Apr.-Nov., $75-180 pp) promises incredible views of the glistening lake, plus a pro shop and seasonal restaurant in the Nantucket-style clubhouse.

For a somewhat less challenging golf game, stop by **Pirate's Cove Adventure Park** (1710 US-31 N, 231/938-9599, www.piratescove.net, 10am-11pm daily Apr.-Oct., $7.95 adults, $7.50 children), where families can play at one of the finest miniature-golf chains in the country. At this award-winning theme park, players can learn about infamous pirates while navigating their way through caves, over footbridges, beneath cascading waterfalls, and alongside wrecked pirate ships. The complex offers two 18-hole courses in addition to bumper boats, racing go-carts, and a water coaster.

Hiking and Biking

Here's the happy general rule about the Traverse Bay region: Downhill ski resorts seem to morph into golf resorts, and cross-country skiing trails often become mountain biking trails.

As proof, the **Pere Marquette State Forest** has a couple of "pathways" in the Traverse City area that double as cross-country and mountain biking trails. You may hike them, too, of course. Most widely known is the 15.6-mile

North American VASA Trail (www.vasa.org). The VASA (named after Swedish King Gustav Vasa) has challenging climbs and descents. Take US-31 toward Acme, turn right onto Bunker Hill Road, drive 1.5 miles, then turn right again onto Bartlett to reach the trailhead. The **Sand Lakes Quiet Area** is a classic northwoods area of small lakes, forest, and meadow about 10 miles east of Traverse City. Ten miles of trails loop through the 2,500 acres of terrain, which is moderately hilly—pleasant, but nothing extreme. For more information on biking, hiking, and camping in the Pere Marquette State Forest, call or stop by the **Michigan Department of Natural Resources's district office** (970 Emerson Rd., 231/922-5280).

For getting around Traverse City and reaching various trailheads on your bike, you can avoid busy US-31 by using the 10.5-mile **Traverse Area Recreation Trail** (TART, www.traversetrails.org). This off-road path shares a railroad right-of-way. It currently extends from US-72 at the West Bay beach to the Acme area, with plans to continue expanding it eastward.

The entire Traverse region offers fantastic back-road cycling. The **Cherry Capital Cycling Club** (231/941-2453, www.cherrycapitalcyclingclub.org) has mapped out zillions of options on its *Bicycle Map of Northwest Michigan*, printed on coated stock that can take a lot of abuse. It's available for $7 at local bike shops like **Brick Wheels** (736 E. 8th St., 231/947-4274, www.brickwheels.com, daily). This full-service shop has knowledgeable employees and rents road bikes, mountain bikes, and in-line skates.

Bird-Watching

A few miles south of Traverse City on Cass Road, the **Grand Traverse Nature Education Reserve** maintains 435 acres along the Boardman River and the Sabin and Boardman Ponds. Though just outside of town, this surprisingly peaceful area includes five miles of self-guided nature trails (no bikes) that wind along the river and cross through marshes and grasslands. The Traverse Bay region attracts particularly large populations of mute swans, and a pair frequently nests here, gliding gracefully across the glassy ponds. Farther upstream on the Boardman, large stands of oak crown a steep bluff climbing up from the river and another small flowage, **Brown Bridge Pond.** Stairs and trails lead out to observation platforms and down to the water's edge.

Canoeing and Fishing

What's that island in the West Arm, you ask? It's **Power Island,** a 200-acre nature preserve owned by the city, with beaches and five miles of hiking trails. For paddlers and other boaters, it's a fun destination for an afternoon picnic, but on weekends, it often becomes a local party spot.

Grand Traverse Bay isn't the only show in town. The beautiful **Boardman River** twists gently through Grand Traverse County before melting into the West Arm at Traverse City. The Boardman offers excellent fly-fishing and canoeing. Generally, its upper stretches run deeper and are better for paddling.

Skiing

West of Thompsonville on M-115, **Crystal Mountain** (12500 Crystal Mountain Dr., 231/378-2623, www.crystalmountain.com) began as a downhill skiing destination but has evolved into much more. While it still offers plenty of downhill—45 runs on two camel-humped slopes—it really shines in the cross-country department. Nordic skiers ride a chairlift from the Nordic Center to the top of the downhill slopes, where a trailhead leads to 25 miles of impeccably groomed cross-country terrain—a combination of gentle pathways and roller-coaster rides that weave all over the resort's 1,500 acres of land. The network is truly one of the finest in the Midwest.

Crystal Mountain invested wisely in its architecture, with pretty villas and tasteful condos scattered all around the property. Rates begin at about $120 but vary widely depending on unit and time of visit. Ski or golf packages are usually your best deal. In summer, Crystal's 36 holes of golf are the main draw, but it also offers clay tennis courts, indoor

© TRAVERSE CITY TOURISM

Ranch Rudolf near the Boardman River

and outdoor pools, and other resort amenities. Some of those great cross-country trails welcome mountain bikes in spring—more than 10 miles of intermediate and advanced terrain overlooking the Betsie River Valley, along with 13 more miles in the nearby state forest.

ACCOMMODATIONS

The Traverse City area has more than 5,000 rooms, everything from inexpensive motels to deluxe resorts. The **Traverse City Tourism** (101 W. Grandview Pkwy., 231/947-1120, www.visittraversecity.com) has a good directory and can help you narrow down your choices. In summer months, you'd be wise to show up with a reservation.

Lots of mom-and-pop motels and chain operations line US-31 along East Bay, Traverse City's original tourist stretch, known as the "miracle mile." Some newer ones have nudged onto this desirable real estate, like the **Pointes North Beachfront Resort Hotel** (2211 US-31 N, 800/968-3422, www.pointesnorth.com, $150-289 d). It has 300 feet of private beach, a waterfront pool, balconies, and in-room mini-kitchens. You'll save money by staying on the other side of US-31, of course, and plenty of

public beaches mean you can still get to the water easily enough. The **Traverse Bay Inn** (2300 US-31 N, 800/968-2646, www.traversebayhotels.com, $149-199 d) is a tidy and pleasant older motel, with an outdoor hot tub and pool, and some fancier new suites with kitchens and fireplaces. It gets bonus points for allowing dogs.

It's not on the water, but the upper floors of the **❰ Park Place Hotel** (300 E. State St., 231/946-5000, www.park-place-hotel.com, $105-276 d) come with incredible views of Grand Traverse Bay. This 1870s downtown landmark was in sad disrepair in 1989, when the local Rotary club purchased it and poured $10 million into renovations. (The Traverse City Rotary is believed to be the wealthiest in the nation, after it discovered oil on property it owned.) The club did a fabulous job restoring the Park Place to its turn-of-the-20th-century opulence.

Outside of town, the pet-friendly, year-round **Ellis Lake Resort** (8440 US-31 S, Interlochen, 231/276-9502, www.ellislakeresort.com, $78-249 d) offers cozy, smoke-free cabins housing private bathrooms and fully equipped kitchens, just 10 minutes from Traverse City. Built in 1939, the cabins are definitely in need of renovation, but some guests appreciate the rustic nature of the place, including the private outdoor yards equipped with picnic tables and campfire pits. While here, guests can enjoy an outdoor hot tub, a small playground, and a variety of other activities, from croquet and volleyball to hiking and snowshoeing. There's also a private 70-acre lake with a swimming beach; guests are also free to use the resort's canoes, rowboats, and paddleboat, and anglers may appreciate the bounty of bass, perch, bluegill, and pike here. Of course, if you're a light sleeper, you probably won't be happy at Ellis Lake; despite the bucolic setting, the property lies very close to the highway. **Ranch Rudolf** (6841 Brown Bridge Rd., Traverse City, 231/947-9529, www.ranchrudolf.com, $68-150 d) has motel units and a lodge with fireplaces, but the draw here is the location: 12 miles from Traverse City in the Pere Marquette State Forest on the shores of the Boardman River. There's paddling and fly-fishing right outside the door. Tent and RV sites are also available.

To the east of Traverse City, golfers and relaxation-seekers often flock to the **Grand Traverse Resort and Spa** (100 Grand Traverse Village Blvd., Acme, 231/534-6000 or 800/236-1577, www.grandtraverseresort.com, $135-439 d), a 900-acre spread that offers access to three signature golf courses, three unique restaurants, a sports bar, a wine-tasting room, a luxurious spa, a health club, a private beach, several swimming pools, and a wide range of well-appointed rooms, suites, condominiums, and resort homes. Given such amenities, plus stunning area views and a complimentary shuttle service to the nearby Turtle Creek Casino & Hotel, it's no wonder that the Grand Traverse Resort is also a popular spot for weddings.

Camping

You won't find a quiet nature retreat, but if you're looking for clean and convenient camping, then **Traverse City State Park** (1132 US-31 N, 231/922-5270, annual $11 Recreation Passport for Michigan residents or $8.40 day-use fee/$30.50 yearly Recreation Passport for nonresidents required) fits the bill. Just two miles east of downtown, the park has 343 modern sites ($27 daily) in a suburbanish setting, grassy with shade trees. A pedestrian overpass will get you across busy US-31 to the main feature of the park: a grassy picnic area and a quarter mile of beach on Grand Traverse Bay. Though pretty, the stretch of sand can quickly become unpleasantly jammed on a summer weekend. Camp here for convenience, maybe, but head elsewhere for a day at the beach—the region has plenty of better choices. For reservations at the state park campground, contact the **Michigan Department of Natural Resources** (800/447-2757, www.michigan. gov/dnr).

You'll find more peace and seclusion at the many rustic campgrounds in the **Pere Marquette State Forest** just a few miles east of town. One to consider is **Arbutus Lake 4** (231/922-5280, $15 daily), with 50 sites on a pretty chain of lakes. From US-31 near the state park, take Four Mile Road south to North Arbutus Road.

FOOD

Traverse City is thick with good restaurants, from simple to elegant. **Apache Trout Grill** (13671 S. West Bay Shore Dr., 231/947-7079, www.apachetroutgrill.com, 10am-10pm daily, $8.50-28) is a casual spot overlooking the West Arm, featuring "northern waters" fish specialties partnered with distinctive sauces.

Sieder's Family Tavern (717 Randolph St., 231/947-9213, www.sleders.com, 11am-11pm Mon.-Thurs., 11am-midnight Fri.-Sat., noon-9pm Sun., $8-17) has been around since 1882, an institution known for its burgers and ribs, and its gorgeous original mahogany and cherry bar.

On the Old Mission Peninsula, the **Boathouse Restaurant** (14039 Peninsula Dr., 231/223-4030, www.boathouseonwestbay. com, 4pm-9pm Mon.-Thurs., 4pm-10pm Fri.-Sun., $36-75) is one of the region's most highly touted restaurants, with fine, diverse cuisine in a nautical atmosphere overlooking the Bowers Harbor marina. The nearby 《 **Mission Table at Bowers Harbor Inn** (13512 Peninsula Dr., 231/223-4222, www.missiontable.net, 5pm-9pm Sun.-Thurs., 5pm-10pm Fri.-Sat., $20-36) offers elegant dining in an 1880s mansion, complete with a resident ghost and an excellent wine list. Specialties include pan-seared diver scallops and smoked jowl.

For something quite different, try the Asian-inspired **Red Ginger** (237 E. Front St., 231/944-1733, www.eatatginger.com, 5pm-10pm Mon.-Thurs., 5pm-11pm Fri.-Sat., $9-32). Featuring flavors from Chinese, Thai, Vietnamese, Japanese, and other Asian cuisines, the Red Ginger is easily the best Asian restaurant in northern Michigan. If you go on a Monday, you can enjoy some live jazz while dining on Red Ginger dragon rolls and sake-glazed sea bass.

INFORMATION AND SERVICES

For more information about Traverse City, contact the **Traverse City Tourism** (101 W. Grandview Pkwy., 231/947-1120, www.visittraversecity.com, 8am-9pm Mon.-Fri., 9am-5pm Sat., noon-6pm Sun.). Stop by the visitors center to pick up maps and brochures, talk to a volunteer staff member about area activities, and check out rotating exhibits that feature the area's culture, history, and environment. You can also consult the **Traverse City Area Chamber of Commerce** (202 E. Grandview Pkwy., 231/947-5075, www.tcchamber.org). For regional news and events, pick up a copy of the **Traverse City Record-Eagle** (www.record-eagle.com) or **Traverse** magazine (www.mynorth.com).

To learn more about the Old Mission Peninsula, visit www.oldmission.com. For details about Benzie County, contact the **Benzie County Visitors Bureau** (826 Michigan Ave., Benzonia, 800/882-5801, www.visitbenzie.com, 9am-5pm Mon.-Fri.).

As Northwest Michigan's largest town, Traverse City offers an assortment of necessary services, including groceries, laundries, banks, and post offices. In case of an emergency requiring police, fire, or ambulance services, dial **911** from any cell or public phone. For medical assistance, consult **Munson Healthcare** (www.munsonhealthcare.org), which offers

several locations in the area, including **Munson Medical Center** (1105 6th St., Traverse City, 231/935-5000).

GETTING THERE AND AROUND

As with many towns and cities throughout Michigan, there are several ways to reach Traverse City. One option is to fly into **Cherry Capital Airport** (TVC, 727 Fly Don't Dr., Traverse City, 231/947-2250, www.tvcairport.com), which offers service from Detroit and Minneapolis on Delta Air Lines and from Chicago on American Airlines and United Airlines. From there, you can hire a taxi from **Cherry Capital Cab** (231/941-8294, www.cherrycapitalcab.com), a 24-hour company that charges $2.40 per pickup, plus $2.80 per mile. Typically, each trip costs an extra $1 for each passenger beyond the first two, and there's also a $5 fee for each pet or bike on-board, not to mention a stopping charge of $0.60 per minute. As an alternative, you can also rent a vehicle from one of five national rental car companies stationed at the airport, which lies about four miles southeast of downtown Traverse City.

Given its location on Grand Traverse Bay, it's also possible to access Traverse City via boat. A journey via bus is also an option. After all, both **Greyhound** (231/946-5180 or 800/231-2222, www.greyhound.com) and **Indian Trails** (800/292-3831, www.indiantrails.com) provide regular service to the **Bay Area Transportation Authority** (BATA, 115 Hall St., 231/941-2324 or 231/778-1025, www.bata.net, one-way $1.50-3 adults, $0.75-1.50 seniors 60 and over, students, and disabled individuals), which, in turn, offers year-round public transportation throughout Grand Traverse and Leelanau Counties. Of course, Traverse City is also a friendly town toward bikers and pedestrians. Many travelers, however, depend on their vehicles to reach the Cherry Capital and explore its environs, and luckily, you can reach the region's biggest town from a variety of directions. From Sault Ste. Marie, for instance, you can simply take I-75 South, cross the Mackinac Bridge (for which you'll have to pay a toll), and merge onto

US-31 South, which will take you directly to Traverse City; without traffic, the 160-mile trip will take about three hours. From downtown Detroit, meanwhile, you can take I-375 North, merge onto I-75 North, follow the I-75 Business Route to M-72 West, and continue onto US-31 South; without traffic, the 256-mile trip will require about four hours.

If, conversely, you're headed from Chicago, just follow I-90 East and I-94 East through Illinois and Indiana, cross the Michigan state line, continue onto I-196 North/US-31 North and I-196 East, merge onto US-131 North toward Cadillac, and take M-113 West and various surface streets to downtown Traverse City; without traffic, the 318-mile trip should take less than five hours. Just be advised that, en route from the Windy City, parts of I-90 East and I-94 East serve as the Indiana Toll Road.

◖ INTERLOCHEN CENTER FOR THE ARTS

South of town, the summertime bustle of Traverse City quickly fades into rolling farmland and woodlots. Incongruously tucked within this rural landscape, 14 miles southwest of Traverse City on M-137, the **Interlochen Center for the Arts** (4000 M-137, Interlochen, 231/276-7200, www.interlochen.org) operates a renowned school on a 1,200-acre campus under a tall canopy of pines. For over 85 years, Interlochen has cultivated a passion for the arts, with year-round programs for adults and a yearly summer camp for young artists, during which nearly 2,500 gifted students come to explore music, dance, theater, film, literature, and visual arts. Audiences can also appreciate Interlochen; throughout the year, this acclaimed institute offers hundreds of concerts, readings, dance and theatrical performances, film screenings, and art exhibitions. Its lineup of musicians and entertainers has always been diverse and impressive, ranging from Itzhak Perlman to the Neville Brothers.

INTERLOCHEN STATE PARK

Not far from the Interlochen school, 187-acre **Interlochen State Park** (M-137,

231/276-9511, annual $11 Recreation Passport for Michigan residents or $8.40 day-use fee/$30.50 yearly Recreation Passport for non-residents required) fans out between Green Lake and Duck Lake, preserving one of the area's few remaining stands of virgin white pine. Thanks to the park's location near Traverse City and Interlochen, its campsites are the main draw. They're very nice ones, too, clustered around the lakeshores with many nice lake views. The modern campground, with the bulk of the park's 480 campsites, is on Duck Lake. Several dozen rustic sites are across the park on Green Lake. Both fill up in summer, so reserve a site ahead of time. For reservations, call 800/447-2757 or visit www.michigan.gov/dnr.

BENZIE COUNTY

Unspoiled Benzie County stretches from west of Traverse City to the port of Frankfort, a hilly region dotted with lakes and bisected by two pristine rivers, the Platte and the Betsie.

The six miles of trails in the **Lake Ann Pathway** offer plenty to see, taking you past Lake Ann, some smaller lakes, a stretch of the Platte River, bogs, and natural springs. The hilly terrain is pleasant for hiking, mountain biking, or cross-country skiing. Part of the Pere Marquette State Forest, it also has a very nice rustic campground with 30 shady, grass-covered sites and a swimming beach on Lake Ann. Follow US-31 west from Traverse City to Reynolds Road (4.5 miles past the turnoff to Interlochen). Turn right and drive 4 miles to the campground and trailheads.

The **Betsie River** wanders across Benzie County, eventually growing into a broad bay at Frankfort. Popular among anglers for trout and lake salmon, it is also a pretty paddling spot. From a put-in at Grass Lake, it's a 44-mile float to Betsie Lake near the Lake Michigan shore, largely through undeveloped state forest. There are several other public launches for a shorter trip.

West of Benzonia, the Betsie passes through the private wildlife sanctuary of **Gwen Frostic Prints** (231/882-5505, www.gwenfrostic.com,

9am-4:30pm Mon.-Sat., 10am-4pm Sun., free). Frostic's studio is an eclectic building of wood, stone, glass, and cement, where a dozen old Heidelberg presses clank away, cranking out Frostic's woodblock prints and poetry. Frostic, who died in 2001, was a woman of bold spirit, whose works paid homage to nature and independence. This intriguing shop has note cards, books, and more.

At Frankfort, the Betsie River flows into Betsie Lake, which forms a remarkably well-protected harbor in Lake Michigan. A crude wooden cross at the river's mouth marks the site of French explorer Père Jacques Marquette's death in 1675. Researchers now believe that the French voyageurs who wrote in their journals of the "Rivière du Père Marquette" were describing the Betsie. From here, you might be able to spot the offshore **Frankfort North Breakwater Light.**

North of Frankfort at Point Betsie, the 1858 **Point Betsie Lighthouse** (231/352-7644 or 231/352-7666, www.pointbetsie.org, 10:30am-4:30pm Sat., 12:30pm-4:30pm Sun., $4 adults, $2 children) perches atop a dune, with waves practically lapping at its base, a tenuous but highly scenic setting. The lighthouse was automated in 1984. The **Zetterberg Preserve at Point Betsie** stretches south from the lighthouse, 71 acres of wonderfully undeveloped duneland, with barren sand beach, scrubby pines, and low-lying dunes.

The Leelanau Peninsula

A ragged land of hills, lakes, and scribbled shoreline straggling northward between Lake Michigan and Grand Traverse Bay, the Leelanau Peninsula has long held a grip on writers and artists (novelist Jim Harrison, among others, makes his home here). Maybe it's the dramatic dichotomy of the place: On its western shore, the oh-so-grand dunes, rising directly up from the lake's surface; inland, a soft and pretty landscape, a muted watercolor of red barns, white farmhouses, and Queen Anne's lace waving in the roadside ditches.

All kinds of people will tell you that Leelanau is an Indian word meaning "land of delights," a description that certainly fits this varied peninsula. The only problem is, the word never existed in the language of the area's Ottawa Indians; they never even used the letter "L." Henry Schoolcraft, the white man who explored the Lake Michigan coast in the 1820s, most likely named it, giving it an "Indian-sounding" name. "Leelanau" can be anything you want it to be—just like your time here.

Leelanau County begins just west of Traverse City, and the county line stretches 30 miles straight west to the Sleeping Bear Dunes and Lake Michigan. Everything above that line is the Leelanau, a 28-mile-long peninsula that includes 98 miles of Great Lakes shoreline, 142 inland lakes and ponds, 58 miles of streams, and numerous award-winning wineries. Roads twist along with the contours of the hills, luring you toward farm stands and onto dirt roads that can't possibly go anywhere you intended to go.

As local author Bill Mulligan has noted, "The meandering expanse of water, woods, and sand of Leelanau is a nice counterweight to the exuberance of Traverse City." So meander.

🄲 SLEEPING BEAR DUNES NATIONAL LAKESHORE

Glaciers and a millennium of wind and water sculpted the Sleeping Bear Dunes, rimming this corner of Michigan with a crust of sand and gravel, like salt on a margarita glass. Beach dunes line the southern part of the national seashore, the classic hillocks of sand you might picture when you think of dunes, created by the prevailing west winds carrying sand to low-lying shores.

But it's the perched dunes that claim center stage here, immense pyramids of sand spiking

THE LEELANAU PENINSULA

up from the very edge of Lake Michigan and climbing at an impossible angle toward the sky. Glaciers first carried these mountains of sand and gravel to what is now the shoreline; nature continues the process, with waves eroding the great dunes and westerlies building them up again. At their highest, the perched dunes once topped out at about 600 feet. Today, Sleeping Bear measures closer to 400 feet, still the largest freshwater dune in the world.

To borrow an old cliché, words really *can't* describe the Sleeping Bear Dunes. They can be a sunny, friendly playground, with squealing children tumbling down the Dune Climb. They can be lunar-like and desolate, a bleak desert on a January day. They can be pale and white-hot at noon, then glow in peaches and pinks like white zinfandel at sunset.

But they are always spectacular. Today, the **Sleeping Bear Dunes National Lakeshore** (9922 Front St., Empire, 231/326-5134, www. nps.gov/slbe, visitors center 8am-6pm daily Memorial Day-Labor Day, 8:30am-4pm daily early Sept.-late May, dunes 24 hours daily, $10

© DANIEL MARTONE

the popular Dune Climb in Sleeping Bear Dunes National Lakeshore

vehicles, $5 individuals, children under 16 free), established in 1977, encompasses nearly 72,000 acres, including 35 miles of Lake Michigan shoreline, North and South Manitou Islands, lakes, rivers, beech and maple forest, waving dune grasses, and those unforgettable dunes. It's truly a magnificent landscape, unlike anything else on the continent.

Empire Area

Situated beside Lake Michigan, Empire is home to the state's newest lighthouse, the cylindrical **Robert Manning Memorial Lighthouse,** erected in 1991 to honor a longtime resident. South of Empire, the **Empire Bluff Trail** winds through forest before erupting into a clearing, for a dramatic vantage point of the big dunes some 5 miles north. In 0.75 mile, the trail dead-ends at a high bluff overlooking the water, so clear you can often see schools of big lake trout. Farther south, **Platte River Point** improves on a great day at the beach with a perfect setting, a sandy spit bordered by Lake Michigan and the mouth of the Platte

River. Rent an inner tube from **Riverside Canoe Trips** (5042 Scenic Hwy., Honor, 231/325-5622, www.canoemichigan.com, 8am-7pm daily) on M-22 at the Platte River Bridge and enjoy the popular sport of launching in the river and shooting out into the lake.

Pierce Stocking Scenic Drive

"I used to have a recurrent nightmare that there was a big highway across the top of the dunes and at the topmost point, a Holiday Inn," writes Kathleen Stocking in *Letters from the Leelanau*. "Now, except for the Holiday Inn, that prescient dream has materialized."

Ironically, the drive is named for Stocking's father, a lumberman who owned much of the land that is now a national park. For those of us who didn't grow up with the dunes as our backyard, this 7.4-mile paved loop that winds through the woods and atop a stretch of dune is less offensive. In fact, it could be argued that it keeps people from traipsing over fragile dune plants for views. Either way, the extremely

LEGEND OF THE SLEEPING BEAR

According to the Ojibwa Indians that formerly inhabited the Great Lakes region, a terrible forest fire once raged in what is now Wisconsin, along the shores of Lake Michigan. In an effort to flee the conflagration, a mother bear and her two cubs tried to swim across the enormous lake, toward present-day Michigan. When the mother reached the far shore, she climbed to the top of a bluff to await her cubs, who had grown tired and lagged behind.

As she waited, the sands collected around her, creating Sleeping Bear Dune, the largest in what eventually became **Sleeping Bear Dunes National Lakeshore** in 1977. Though the cubs sadly drowned in the lake, the Great Spirit took pity on the grieving mother and raised her children from the depths as North and South Manitou Islands, which lie offshore and are also part of the national park.

popular route *is* there, with scenic overlooks of Glen Lake, the dunes, and Lake Michigan.

The drive offers access to the **Cottonwood Trail,** a 1.5-mile, sandy, self-guided walk that educates visitors about the ecology and diverse plant life in the dunes. The drive also leads you to the **Lake Michigan Overlook,** a platform 450 feet above the water with views stretching to Point Betsie, 15 miles south, and 54 miles across to Wisconsin. Though the park service discourages it—having seen too many sprained ankles, broken arms, and close cardiac calls— you can slide your way down the dune here, though it's a steep, long, exhausting climb back up, about an hour's worth of crawling.

That's why the park service points visitors instead to the nearby **Dune Climb,** a more manageable 130-foot dune that Mother Nature conveniently deposited on the lee side of the plateau. It's the perfect place to let kids run off their energy, or to climb up for a fine view of shimmering Glen Lake. Even hardier souls can continue on the **Dunes Trail,** a challenging, 3.5-mile hike that extends from the Dune Climb, across several rugged dunes, to the sandy shores of Lake Michigan and back.

Glen Haven Area

In sleepy Glen Haven, the park service operates a nifty museum in the old lifesaving station. In summer months, the **Sleeping Bear Point Coast Guard Station Maritime Museum** (11am-5pm daily mid-May-Sept., noon-5pm

Sat.-Sun. Oct., free) depicts the work of the U.S. Lifesaving Service, the forerunner of the U.S. Coast Guard. Exhibits include lifesaving boats and the cannon used to shoot lifelines out to the sinking vessels, while video programs illustrate the drill and the rigorous life the crews led. They got a regular workout: Some 50 ships wrecked along this passage between the mainland and the nearby Manitou Islands, one of the busiest routes on the Great Lakes in the mid-19th century, since it offered a convenient shortcut between Mackinac Island and Chicago. The station originally sat a few miles west at Sleeping Bear Point, but was moved here in 1931 when the ever-omnipotent dunes threatened to bury it.

East on M-109, **Glen Arbor** occupies a small patch of private real estate completely surrounded by the national park, Lake Michigan, and Glen Lake. It caters to the tourist trade with mostly tasteful galleries and craft shops, and also has a grocery for reloading the picnic supplies. Cherry lovers shouldn't miss **Cherry Republic** (6026 Lake St., 800/206-6949, www.cherryrepublic.com, 9am-9pm daily), which bills itself as "the largest exclusive retailer of cherry products in the United States." You'll find cherry baked goods, cherry sodas, chocolate-covered cherries, cherry salsas, cherry jam . . . well, you get the idea.

Near Glen Arbor, the **Pyramid Point** hiking trail is a hilly 2.7-mile loop that leads to the park's northernmost point, with a high lookout

KERRY KELLY/NPS

Glen Haven

over Lake Michigan and Sleeping Bear Bay. To reach the trailhead, take M-22 three miles east of Glen Arbor to Port Oneida Road.

North and South Manitou Islands

Lying about 17 miles off the mainland, the Manitous comprise more than 20,000 acres of once-developed land that has largely been reclaimed by nature and now is managed as part of Sleeping Bear Dunes National Lakeshore. South Manitou is the smaller (5,260 acres) and more accessible of the two, serviced by passenger ferry from Leland daily in summer months. The same ferry also stops at North Manitou five times a week in July and August, fewer times in spring and fall. The trip to either island takes about 90 minutes. No cars, bikes, or pets are permitted. For schedule information and reservations, contact **Manitou Island Transit** (Leland, 231/256-9061, www.leelanau. com/manitou, round-trip $35 adults, $20 children under 13). The islands have potable water at a few locations, but no other services. Even day hikers should pack a lunch.

South Manitou Island was first settled in the 1830s. Islanders made a living by farming and logging, supplying food and fuel to the wood-burning steamers that traveled through the busy Manitou Passage. Farming was exceptional on South Manitou. Isolated from alien pollens, it proved the perfect place to produce crops and experiment with hybrid seeds, and was soon highly respected in agricultural circles. A South Manitou rye crop won first prize in an international exposition in 1920; by the 1940s, most of Michigan's bean crop came from South Manitou seed. By the 1960s, though, the island had become mostly a summer cottage getaway, and, a decade later, the National Park Service began condemning and buying up the land for a national lakeshore.

Today, visitors can arrange for a tour ($8 adults, $5 children) through the ferry company, a 90-minute trip in an open-air truck that follows abandoned roads to farmsteads, a schoolhouse, and a cemetery. Near the ferry dock, a small visitors center in the old village post office has displays on island history. Nearby,

© DANIEL MARTONE

the original Cherry Republic in Glen Arbor

the 1872 **South Manitou Island Lighthouse** is open on summer afternoons, allowing you to scale the 100-foot tower.

Hikers and backpackers will want to get farther afield, though. The island has 10 miles of marked hiking trails that lead to some interesting sights. Day hikers will have to move right along, but they can make the 6-mile round-trip to check out the wreck of the *Francisco Morazan* and still make it back in time for the afternoon ferry. Like many ships that failed to navigate the tricky Manitou Passage, this Liberian freighter ran aground in 1960. Its battered skeleton lies largely above the water's surface, just a few hundred yards offshore.

Nearby, a side trail winds through a grove of virgin cedars, some more than 500 years old. Deemed too isolated to log, the slow-growing trees are the largest of their kind left in North America, some measuring more than 15 feet around and nearly 90 feet tall. Another half mile west, the state's most remote dunes tower over the western shore, 300-foot perched dunes similar to those on the mainland.

To properly enjoy all the island has to offer, of course, you need to spend more than an afternoon. Camping is permitted only at three rustic campsites; reservations are required.

Like South Manitou, **North Manitou Island** was once a farming and logging community, then a summer getaway. Acquired by the National Park Service in 1984, it still has some patches of private property. But otherwise, this large island is even less developed than its southern neighbor. Those who come here do so to camp, hike, and explore the abandoned buildings.

North Manitou receives far fewer visitors than South Manitou—until fall hunting season, anyway. Nine deer were introduced in the 1920s in the hopes of developing a herd large enough to hunt. Boy, did that work! In 1981, more than 2,000 deer roamed the island, decimating the vegetation so much that the island's forests had an "open park-like appearance," according to the park service. Today, it manages the herd by issuing hunting permits.

North Manitou has only one water source

© DANIEL MARTONE

Leland's historic "Fishtown" district

and one small rustic campground near the ferry dock; backcountry camping is permitted throughout the island's public property. Backcountry permits, though free, are required.

For camping permits and more information on the Manitous, contact **Sleeping Bear Dunes National Lakeshore** (231/326-5134, www.nps.gov/slbe).

LELAND TO NORTHPORT

The restored **"Fishtown"** at Leland's harbor is probably one of the most photographed spots in all of Michigan, a collection of 19th-century weathered gray fish shanties lined on the docks. Whether you find it charming or obnoxious pretty much pegs your feelings about development—or reveals you as a local who remembers what the harbor looked like before the gift shops came to town. For many Leelanau residents, slicked-up Leland is a sad commentary on how tourism is erasing a simpler lifestyle.

Leland was a diverse industrial center in the mid-1800s, with two sawmills, a gristmill,

an iron smelter, and a flourishing commercial fishing trade. By the early 1900s, eight fisheries were operating out of Leland. Where the Carp River spills into Lake Michigan, they built shanties along the docks, which they used to store ice, repair nets, and house equipment. Once common in ports all over the Great Lakes, most of these complexes completely disappeared when commercial fishing declined in the mid-1900s.

In Leland, the shanties happily remain, lined up on the docks right out of a historical photo. **Carlson's Fishery** (205 W. River, 231/256-9801, www.carlsonsfish.com, 9am-6pm daily) still operates here, with its sturdy snub-nosed boats tied up to the pier and a shop that sells fresh fillets and smoked trout out of a long deli case. Most of the other shanties, though, now house gift shops and galleries, and the fishnets dry in the sun solely for the benefit of the summer tourist trade.

Though it's undeniably touristy, Leland is also undeniably attractive. The Carp River rolls by, where you can gaze down at the steelhead schooling in the waters. And whether or not you care for the shops, appreciate the fact that no one tore down these neat old buildings.

East of Leland lies lengthy Lake Leelanau. Popular with anglers, the lake is also a good spot for paddlers, especially at the **Cedar River Preserve** (Leelanau Conservancy, 231/256-9665, www.theconservancy.com) along its southern shore, part of the Pere Marquette State Forest. Launch a canoe partway up the eastern shore, where Lake Leelanau Road intersects Bingham Road.

North of Leland, handsome **Peterson Park** sits high atop a bluff overlooking Lake Michigan, with picnic tables, a playground, and a great vantage point for the area's renowned sunsets. A steep staircase leads to a rocky beach, a good spot to hunt for Petoskey stones. Take M-201 to Peterson Park Road and turn left. For swimming, **Christmas Cove** offers a perfect arc of sugar-sand beach near the tip of the peninsula. To find it, follow M-201 north from Northport; just after it joins CR-640, turn left on Kilcherman Road, which leads to Christmas Cove Road.

With a fine horseshoe harbor in the protected waters of Grand Traverse Bay, it's not surprising that **Northport** was one of the first spots settled on the Leelanau. Catholic missionaries established a village there in 1849, bringing with them several area Ottawa families that they had successfully converted to Christianity. Within 20 years, Northport was the county seat, overseeing a population of 2,500, and had a thriving commercial fishing industry. At the turn of the 20th century, it built a fancy resort hotel with room for 250 guests; within five years, the uninsured building burned to the ground. Today, Northport is popular with pleasure boaters, who still appreciate its snug harbor, and shoppers, who cruise its cute little downtown, a row of revamped 1860s buildings filled with eclectic antiques and clothing shops.

LEELANAU STATE PARK

Split into two units at the tip of the Leelanau Peninsula, the 1,350-acre **Leelanau State Park**

(15310 N. Lighthouse Point Rd., Northport, 231/386-5422 in summer or 231/922-5270 in winter, annual $11 Recreation Passport for Michigan residents or $8.40 day-use fee/$30.50 yearly Recreation Passport for nonresidents required) is a wonderful surprise: While the northern unit, with its lighthouse and campground, is very popular, most visitors seem to ignore its southern portion—meaning you can often have its lovely beaches and trails all to yourself.

In the southern unit, low dunes and more than a mile of sand beach curve along Cathead Bay. It's a mile walk from the parking area through maple and beech forest to get to the water, so it rarely draws a crowd. The park's 8.5 miles of walking trails radiate out from the same parking area. The **Mud Lake Tour** circles a wetland area and small lake, a good choice in spring and fall when waterfowl migrate through the area. The **Lake Michigan Trail** leads to the water, but don't skip the short side trail to the overlook—a stairway climbs up a dune for a breathtaking view of North Manitou Island. To reach the southern unit, follow CR-629 north and turn left just after Woolsey Airport.

Five miles north, the **Grand Traverse Lighthouse** (15500 N. Lighthouse Point Rd., Northport, 231/386-7195, www.grandtraverse-lighthouse.com, 10am-6pm daily June-Aug., noon-4pm daily May and Sept.-Oct., $4 adults, $2 children) presides over the park's northern unit at the peninsula's tip. Built in 1858, the pretty white brick tower looks woefully small for the huge expanse of water that surrounds it. (The Coast Guard thought so, too; the light was decommissioned in 1972, replaced by a more pedestrian—but taller—steel tower churning away down on the beach.) Today, visitors can stroll through the on-site museum or climb the tower when the lighthouse is open.

SUTTONS BAY

Once a town largely inhabited by immigrant laborers from the fruit orchards, Suttons Bay has gotten fancier and wealthier along with the rest of the Leelanau Peninsula. With mechanization, there simply aren't that many laborers anymore, and the desirable real estate—on Grand Traverse Bay, just 12 miles from Traverse City, with views of the cross-hatched orchards of the Old Mission Peninsula—was just too good to leave alone. These days, Suttons Bay has almost become a suburb of Traverse City. Residents have worked hard to maintain the community's own personality, though, with colorfully painted storefronts and old-fashioned red telephone booths along St. Joseph's Avenue (M-22). Suttons Bay's downtown boasts a restored movie theater, all manner of galleries and boutiques, and some of the best restaurants in the Grand Traverse region.

◖ WINERIES OF GRAND TRAVERSE BAY

As on the Old Mission Peninsula, the surrounding waters of Lake Michigan have a moderating effect on the Leelanau Peninsula, providing a surprisingly fruitful climate for growing cherries, apples, peaches, and wine grapes. Slow-changing lake temperatures keep things nice and cool during the growing season; come winter, they insulate the delicate trees and vines from killing deep freezes.

Michigan leads the nation in cherry production, and the Leelanau accounts for a quarter of that crop. And while Michigan's grape harvest isn't yet ready to challenge California's, a few of its wines have been. Leelanau (and Old Mission Peninsula) wineries regularly produce award-winning vintages, especially rieslings, which do particularly well in this climate, and chardonnays. Sure, you can still find some overly sweet cherry wines, but serious vintners are letting their wines do the talking, and winning over new converts every year. Some 25 wineries now make their home on the Leelanau Peninsula, and most offer both tours and tastings. For the latest information about this winemaking region, consult the **Leelanau Peninsula Vintner's Association** (www.lpwines.com).

Leelanau Cellars

Leelanau Cellars (7161 N. West Bay Shore Dr., Omena, 231/386-5201, www.leelanaucellars.com, 10am-6pm Mon.-Sat., noon-6pm

Sun.) is the largest winery on the peninsula, producing 65,000 gallons of vinifera, hybrid, and fruit wines each year. Highest honors go to its Tall Ship chardonnay.

L. Mawby Vineyards

L. Mawby Vineyards (4519 S. Elm Valley Rd., Suttons Bay, 231/271-3522, www.lmawby.com, noon-6pm Thurs.-Sat.) is one of the region's smallest wineries—with a big reputation, especially for its sparkling wines and oak-barrel-fermented dry whites. Larry Mawby produces about 3,000 cases a year, with a goal to "keep things small enough to do what I want to do—make great wine with minimal intervention." He brings a creative flair to the winemaking business, evidenced in the artful wine labels designed by his wife, artist Peggy Core. From Suttons Bay, follow CR-633 south to Elm Valley Road.

Boskydel Vineyard

Boskydel Vineyard (7501 E. Otto Rd., Lake Leelanau, 231/256-7272, www.boskydel.com, noon-6pm daily) was the first vineyard in the Grand Traverse region, with French hybrid grapes first planted in 1964. Today, the winery produces about 2,500 cases a year—mostly semi-dry red and white table wines—from its vineyards sloping down toward Lake Michigan. The winery is two miles south of Lake Leelanau on CR-41.

Good Harbor Vineyards

Some consider Bruce Simpson's dry white chardonnay and pinot gris the finest wines to come out of the Traverse Bay region. An informative self-guided tour at **Good Harbor Vineyards** (34 S. Manitou Trail, 231/256-7165, www.goodharbor.com, 11am-5pm Mon.-Sat., noon-5pm Sun. May-Nov.), three miles south of Leland on M-22 in Lake Leelanau, explains how he's done it.

Chateau Fontaine Vineyards & Winery

Stop by **Chateau Fontaine Vineyards & Winery** (2290 S. French Rd., Lake Leelanau,

NORTHWEST MICHIGAN

© TRAVERSE CITY TOURISM

sampling wines at Black Star Farms

231/256-0000, www.chateaufontaine.com, noon-5pm Wed.-Sun. June-Oct., noon-5pm Sat.-Sun. May and Nov.-Dec.), a long-ago potato farm and cow pasture now transformed into 30 acres of grapevines. They produce chardonnay, pinot gris, and a "Woodland White," among others.

Black Star Farms

In Suttons Bay, you'll find **Black Star Farms** (10844 E. Revold Rd., 231/944-1271, www.blackstarfarms.com, 10am-6pm Mon.-Sat., noon-5pm Sun. May-Nov., 11am-5pm Mon.-Sat., noon-5pm Sun. Dec.-Apr.), billed as "an agricultural destination." This fascinating winery, distillery, creamery, and farmers market also offers a welcoming tasting room and a luxurious bed-and-breakfast.

More Wineries

Take special note of several other locales in Suttons Bay, including **Raftshol Vineyards** (1865 N. West Bay Shore Dr., 231/271-5650,

11am-6pm Mon.-Sat., noon-6pm Sun.), a former dairy enterprise and cherry orchard that now produces over 1,000 cases of bordeaux varietal red wines annually.

Owned by a cardiologist with a special interest in Michigan's agriculture, **Chateau de Leelanau Vineyard & Winery** (5048 S. West Bay Shore Dr., 231/271-8888, www.chateaudeleelanau.com, 11am-6pm Mon.-Sat., noon-5pm Sun. May-Oct., by appointment Mon.-Wed., noon-5pm Thurs.-Sun. Nov.-Apr.) presents a tasting room and retail store not far from Grand Traverse Bay.

Established in 1996, the **Ciccone Vineyard & Winery** (10343 E. Hilltop Rd., 231/271-5553, www.cicconevineyard.com, noon-5pm Sat. Jan.-Mar., noon-5pm Thurs.-Sun. Apr.-May, noon-6pm daily June-Oct., noon-5pm Tues.-Sat. Nov.-Dec.), owned by Madonna's father, is a Tuscan-inspired winery and tasting room. For a $5 fee, you can purchase a Ciccone wine glass and up to five tastings of the vintner's choice.

EVENTS

The Leelanau Peninsula is home to a myriad of art festivals, culinary events, and seasonal gatherings. One curious event occurs in late September, the annual **Harvest Stompede Vineyard Run & Walk,** which features a race through Leelanau's vineyards as well as a tour of area wineries. During the weekend, visitors are able to sample wines, gourmet pastas, and other culinary delights. For more information, consult the **Leelanau Peninsula Vintner's Association** (www.lpwines.com).

DIVING

The waters around North Manitou Island, South Manitou Island, and the Sleeping Bear Dunes are rife with historic dock ruins and shipwrecks, making the **Manitou Passage Underwater Preserve** a fascinating place for scuba divers. Besides the popular *Francisco Morazan* wreck near the south end of South Manitou Island, divers enjoy exploring the artifacts that abound on the *Walter L. Frost*, a wooden steamer that ran aground in 1905, only to be further wrecked in 1960 when the *Morazan* landed on top of it. For more information, contact the **Michigan Underwater Preserve Council** (800/970-8717, www.michiganpreserves.org).

ACCOMMODATIONS AND FOOD

If your budget won't allow a stay at **C Black Star Farms** (10844 E. Revold Rd., Suttons Bay, 231/944-1271, www.blackstarfarms.com, $150-395 d)—a winery, creamery, market, and luxurious B&B—you'll be happy to know that the region also accommodates campers. The rustic campground at **Leelanau State Park** (15310 N. Lighthouse Point Rd., Northport, 231/386-5422 in summer or 231/922-5270 in winter, annual $11 Recreation Passport for Michigan residents or $8.40 day-use fee/$30.50 yearly Recreation Passport for nonresidents required) has 52 wonderful sites ($15 daily), with several right along the water and several more with water views. Though the campground is extremely popular in summer, most sites offer a fair amount of seclusion.

In Leland, a couple of restaurants overlook the river and Fishtown, including **C The Cove** (111 River St., 231/256-9834, www.thecoveleland.com, 11:30am-9pm daily, $9-26), featuring seafood chowder, fish stew, and fresh fish specials. A block or two farther upstream, across M-22 (the main drag), **The Bluebird Restaurant & Bar** (102 River St., 231/256-9081, www.leelanau.com/bluebird, 11:30-9pm Tues.-Sun., $6-14) is a well-known dinner spot, with reasonably priced seafood dishes, homemade soups, and a decent wine list. Meanwhile, Lake Leelanau is home to **Dick's Pour House** (103 W. Philip St., 231/256-9912, www.dickspourhouse.com, 11:30am-10pm Sun.-Thurs., 11:30am-11pm Fri.-Sat. in summer, 11:30am-8pm Sun.-Thurs., 11:30am-9pm Fri.-Sat. in winter, $7-16), where you can sample pizza, sandwiches, soups, pies, and a Friday fish fry.

INFORMATION AND SERVICES

For more information about the Leelanau Peninsula, contact the **Traverse City Convention & Visitors Bureau** (101 W. Grandview Pkwy., 231/947-1120, www.visittraversecity.com, 8am-9pm Mon.-Fri., 9am-5pm Sat., noon-6pm Sun.). You can also consult the **Leelanau Peninsula Chamber of Commerce** (5046 S. West Bay Shore Dr., Ste. G, Suttons Bay, 231/271-9895, www.leelanauchamber.com), **Leelanau Communications** (113 N. Main, Leland, 231/256-2829, www.leelanau.com), the **Leland Michigan Chamber of Commerce** (231/256-0079, www.lelandmi.com), the **Suttons Bay Area Chamber of Commerce** (231/271-5077, www.suttonsbayarea.com), and **The Third Coast Traveler** (www.thetctraveler.com).

If you require other services while traveling across the Leelanau Peninsula, remember that nearby Traverse City offers everything you might need, from groceries to hospitals. If an emergency occurs, don't hesitate to dial **911** from any phone.

GETTING THERE AND AROUND

To reach the Leelanau Peninsula, many travelers first arrive in Traverse City, usually via their own vehicles. Of course, it's also possible to reach Traverse City by flying into **Cherry Capital Airport** (TVC, 727 Fly Don't Dr., Traverse City, 231/947-2250, www.tvcairport.com) or coming by bus via **Greyhound** (231/946-5180 or 800/231-2222, www.greyhound.com) or **Indian Trails** (800/292-3831, www.indiantrails.com). From there, you can then rent a vehicle (or rely on your own) and head west on M-72 to Empire, where you'll find the headquarters of Sleeping Bear Dunes National Lakeshore; the 24-mile trip from Traverse City to Empire usually takes about a half hour. From Traverse City, you can also explore the wineries of the Leelanau Peninsula by heading north on M-22, which actually traces the perimeter of the peninsula, passing through towns like Suttons Bay, Northport, Leland, Glen Arbor, and Empire. To give you an idea of the distances here, know that it takes about 42 minutes to cover the 29 miles between Traverse City and Northport via M-22. Of course, if you'd rather not drive, you can also rely on the **Bay Area Transportation Authority** (BATA, 231/941-2324 or 231/778-1025, www.bata.net, one-way $1.50-3 adults, $0.75-1.50 seniors 60 and over, students, and disabled individuals) to navigate the peninsula.

Manistee to Cadillac

As you continue south along the Lake Michigan shoreline, towns grow sparser, summer crowds thin, and beaches climb into windswept dunes. If you're looking for a quiet beach walk or a mellow waterfront town without a full parade of activities and attractions, this may be the stretch of shore for you. Even farther south lies the Manistee National Forest, which is surrounded by towns like Ludington and Pentwater and contains several inland lakes, miles of hiking possibilities, and a wildflower sanctuary.

MANISTEE

Manistee's slogan is "Manistee: A Great Place to Be." While the city's downtown is a charming mix of historic logging buildings and ornate Victorian mansions, much of the credit for that claim goes to the wonderful Manistee National Forest that lies just outside the city limits. In fact, the national forest is such a part of Manistee's psyche that the city honors it with the annual **Manistee National Forest Festival** each July. Manistee serves as a good base camp for exploring the forest, as well as an

the Manistee North Pierhead Light

© JIM PARKIN | DREAMSTIME.COM

exceptionally lovely and untouched stretch of Lake Michigan shoreline. Before you head south, though, stop by the **Manistee North Pierhead Light,** erected in 1927 and still active today.

LUDINGTON

Because of its midpoint position on Lake Michigan and its ample supply of lumber, Ludington enjoyed a boom as a busy port during the latter half of the 19th century. (Originally named Père Marquette in honor of the missionary explorer who died here in 1675, the city later changed its name to reflect the influence of its more recent founder, James Ludington, a lumber baron.) Today, visitors are drawn to its enormous expanse of sugar-sand beach. As you'll see from the busy marina in the heart of town, fishing and boating are the pulse of this appealing community. Take special note of the white pyramidal lighthouse, the 1924 **Ludington North Pierhead Light,** which replaced a much older lighthouse at the end of the breakwater.

Historic White Pine Villag

Opened in 1976, the **Historic** W... **Village** (1687 S. Lakeshore Dr., 231/843-4808, www.historicwhitepinevillage.org, 10am-5pm Tues.-Sat., 1pm-5pm Sun. Memorial Day-Labor Day, 10am-5pm Tues.-Sat. early-late May and Labor Day-mid-Oct., closed mid-Oct.-Apr., $9 adults, $6 children 6-17, children under 6 free) presents 30 buildings and historic sites, dedicated to preserving Mason County's past. It's worth bringing the whole family for this educational yet fun-filled tour. The old-fashioned ice cream parlor is an especially big hit with young travelers.

⊘ Ludington State Park

Ludington State Park (8800 W. M-116, 231/843-8671, www.ludingtonfriends.com, annual $11 Recreation Passport for Michigan residents or $8.40 day-use fee/$30.50 yearly Recreation Passport for nonresidents required) is one of the state's finest outdoor playgrounds and one of the largest state parks in the Lower

© DANIEL MARTONE

enjoying the waters of Ludington State Park

Peninsula. Attendance ranks in the top 10 of all Michigan state parks, with good reason. The park encompasses more than 5,300 acres of beautiful beaches, almost six miles of Lake Michigan shoreline, dunes and forests that wrap around picnic areas, biking and hiking paths, three campgrounds, an interesting interpretive center, an inland lake, and a canoe trail.

The park occupies a wide strip of land between Lake Michigan and Hamlin Lake, straddling the Big Sable River, which connects them. The numerous trails that lace the park's interior are among the finest foot paths in the Lower Peninsula. They offer everything from a leisurely half-hour stroll to a rather strenuous six-mile round-trip trek to the 1867 **Big Sable Point Lighthouse** (www.bigsablelighthouse.org, 10am-5pm daily May-Oct., $2 adults, $1 children 12-18), painted in tiers of black and white, and standing guard over Big Sable Point. Trudging through sand is tiring on the calves, but the view from the top of the tower makes it all worth it.

PENTWATER AND SILVER LAKE

Once considered a sleepy town along the Lake Michigan shore, the Victorian logging town of Pentwater ticks along at a pleasant—but not frantic—summer pace. On Hancock Street, Pentwater's main drag, visitors prowl through a growing number of antiques shops, searching for turn-of-the-20th-century treasures and nautical artifacts. A parade of pleasure boats purr through the boat channel that links Pentwater Lake and Lake Michigan, accompanied by folks strolling along the Channel Lane Park walkway. On the north side of the boat channel, **Charles Mears State Park** (400 W. Lowell St., 231/869-2051, annual $11 Recreation Passport for Michigan residents or $8.40 day-use fee/$30.50 yearly Recreation Passport for nonresidents required) seems more like a city beach than a state park.

Between Silver Lake and Lake Michigan lie more than 2,000 acres of unspoiled and ever-shifting sand dunes, remnants of the glaciers that once scrubbed this landscape. They are one of the largest deposits of dunes on the shores of Lake Michigan, acre after acre of ridges and valleys of wind-blown sand that are void of trees, scrub, or, in many places, even dune grass. Most of the dunes are protected as **Silver Lake State Park** (9679 W. State Park Rd., 231/873-3083, annual $11 Recreation Passport for Michigan residents or $8.40 day-use fee/$30.50 yearly Recreation Passport for nonresidents required), with hiking trails that climb high sand hills and weave through grasses and stunted trees. The park and dunes are located on one of the westernmost spots of the state's shoreline, a broad point that extends more than seven miles out from the main shore. From here, you can visit the 1874 **Little Sable Point Light,** a tall brick conical structure preserved by the park.

The Wood family once owned most of this land, and sold it to the state in 1973. They retained the right to use about 700 acres at the park's south end to operate **Mac Wood's Dune Rides** (629 N. 18th Ave., Mears, 231/873-2817, www.macwoodsdunerides.com, daily mid-May-Oct., $17 adults, $11 children 3-11). Visitors load into hybrid buggy/trucks for a seven-mile drive through the dunes, roaring up and down hills and splashing along the Lake Michigan surf line. While it's easy to question this kind of use of the dunes, the operation does make an effort to help visitors understand and appreciate the region's unique ecology.

MANISTEE NATIONAL FOREST

Manistee National Forest (231/775-2421, www.fs.usda.gov) stretches from Manistee south to Muskegon, over a half-million acres of woods, beaches, dunes, and two fine paddling rivers, the Pine and Pere Marquette. Most notable of the national forest's many attractions is the **Nordhouse Dunes Wilderness,** a 3,450-acre swath of untouched dunes and dune forest. It is the only federally designated wilderness in Michigan's Lower Peninsula, and the only federal dune wilderness in the nation.

The wilderness area includes 3 miles of isolated Lake Michigan beach, where dunes reach more than 140 feet. From the beach, 10 miles of hiking trails spin inland. Because they are minimally signed, bring a map and compass, along with plenty of water. Backcountry camping is permitted in the wilderness more than 200 feet from the waterline. The adjacent Nordhouse Dunes Recreation Area offers a modern campground with potable water.

Hikers should seek out the **Manistee River Trail,** a 10-mile route that follows the east bank of the Manistee River. The trail offers plenty of diversity, scaling steep slopes, meandering through pine and hardwood forest, dipping through ferny glades and crossing several creeks. It is open to foot traffic only. The north trailhead is near the south end of the Hodenpyl Dam, which lies east of Manistee. Pick up a map at the **ranger office** (412 Red Apple Rd., Manistee, 231/723-2211).

For paddlers, the **Pine National Scenic River** serves up lots of twists and turns, and some Class II rapids as well. There are four access sites within the national forest, each with toilets, water, grills, and parking areas. Rent canoes from **Horina Canoe & Kayak Rental** (9889 M-37, Wellston, 231/862-3470, www. horinacanoe.com, $42 daily). The wonderfully clear **Pere Marquette River,** also a national scenic river, is great for both canoeing and fishing, with healthy populations of brown trout, steelhead, and salmon. The navigable stretch within the national forest is more than 43 miles long, with several access points.

◖ Loda Lake National Wildflower Sanctuary

Nestled within the Manistee National Forest, between the towns of Brohman and White Cloud, the **Loda Lake National Wildflower Sanctuary** (www.fs.usda.gov/hmnf, 24 hours daily, $5 daily, $15 weekly) is the only sanctuary of its kind ever established in a U.S. national forest. Although the sanctuary is open year-round, it's not maintained in winter, and the ideal months for seeing wildflowers are April-September. During this time, nature lovers can take a self-guided tour through oak-maple woodlands, old pine plantations, and

THE RULES OF LODA LAKE

Situated in Manistee National Forest in the northwestern part of Michigan's Lower Peninsula, **Loda Lake National Wildflower Sanctuary** is the only one of its kind in America's national forest system. Supported by the Federated Garden Clubs of Michigan for more than seven decades, the sanctuary welcomes visitors all year long, though it's particularly popular May-August. While several diversions are allowed here, including hiking, hunting, boating, snowshoeing, and cross-country skiing, certain restrictions do apply. So, bear the following rules in mind on your next visit to Loda Lake:

- Do not bring bicycles, llamas, pack and saddle animals, snowmobiles, and other motorized vehicles into the sanctuary.

- Keep your dogs leashed at all times.

- Remember that hiking and foot travel are only permitted on official trails.

- Do not pick or remove wildflowers.

- Use only dead and down wood for fires.

- Build fires in grills and fire rings only.

- Do not camp overnight in the sanctuary.

For more information about **Loda Lake National Wildflower Sanctuary** (800/821-6263, www.fs.usda.gov/hmnf), contact the **Baldwin/White Cloud Ranger Station** (P.O. Box Drawer D, Baldwin, MI 49304, 231/745-4631).

a shrub swamp, boasting a slew of wildflowers and other plant species, from columbine to witch hazel to huckleberries. A detailed brochure is available from the **Baldwin/White Cloud Ranger District** (650 N. Michigan Ave., Baldwin, 231/745-4631, 8am-4:30pm daily mid-May-mid-Sept., 8am-4:30pm Mon.-Fri. mid-Sept.-mid-May). To reach the sanctuary,

© LODA LAKE NATIONAL WILDFLOWER SANCTUARY

nodding lady's tresses in the Loda Lake National Wildflower Sanctuary

head north from White Cloud on M-37 for 6.8 miles; the sanctuary will be on your left.

CADILLAC

It may share a name with the luxury car maker, but snowmobiles, not Caddies, are the preferred means of transportation in the forest and lake country surrounding Cadillac. An intricate web of trails links the city with routes through the Manistee National Forest. In summer, much of the same crowd turns to fishing. The city of 10,270 sits on the shore of large 1,150-acre Lake Cadillac, which is linked by canal to even larger Lake Mitchell. Both are known for excellent northern pike and walleye fishing. The canal was originally built by loggers, who grew tired of the twisting, shallow river that originally traversed the wetlands between the two lakes.

Situated between the two lakes, **William Mitchell State Park** (6093 E. M-115, Cadillac, 231/775-7911, annual $11 Recreation Passport for Michigan residents or $8.40 day use fee/$30.50 yearly Recreation Passport for non-residents required) is a dream come true for anglers and pleasure boaters. Some of its 221 modern campsites ($27-29 daily) are in fact on the canal itself, where boats can be tied up right next to your tent or RV. The park maintains a boat launch on Lake Cadillac, as well as swimming beaches on both lakes. There's a short nature trail skirting a wetlands area with an observation tower. Visit early in the morning to observe the active birds here. Though it's pretty, be aware that this park and both of its lakes tend to be extremely busy throughout the summer. Those looking for a peaceful retreat will likely be disappointed by the buzz of activity, but if that doesn't scare you away, be sure to reserve a spot well in advance by calling 800/447-2757 or visiting www.michigan.gov/dnr.

GOLF

Situated in Mecosta County, east of Manistee National Forest and accessible via US-131, the courses of **The Resorts of Tullymore & St. Ives** (9900 St. Ives Dr., Stanwood, 231/972-4837, www.tullymoregolf.com, daily Apr.-Oct., $75-160 pp) are popular among golfers of all skill levels. This fine resort, which you'll find on the road between Grand Rapids and Cadillac, offers two marvelous 18-hole courses, an Irish pub, and two fine restaurants.

ACCOMMODATIONS

In Manistee, the **Days Inn** (1462 US-31 S, 231/723-8385, www.daysinn.com, $92-115 d) offers an indoor pool and spa, and a nice location at the south end of town near the scenic riverwalk. Just steps from Lake Michigan and downtown Ludington, **Snyder's Shoreline Inn** (903 W. Ludington Ave., 231/845-1261, www.snydersshoreinn.com, mid-May-Oct., $59-309 d) offers a variety of rooms and cottages. ⊏ **The Lamplighter Bed & Breakfast** (602 E. Ludington Ave., Ludington, 231/843-9792, www.ludington-michigan.com, $125-170 d) is a Victorian-inspired inn housed within an 1894 home, with five guest rooms and original paintings, lithographs, and antiques throughout. On Hamlin Lake, **Sauble Resort** (3443

N. Stearns, Ludington, 231/843-8497, www. saubleresort.com, $67-165 d) presents housekeeping cottages overlooking the dunes, not far from Ludington State Park.

Camping

Ludington State Park (8800 W. M-116, 231/843-2423, annual $11 Recreation Passport for Michigan residents or $8.40 day-use fee/$30.50 yearly Recreation Passport for nonresidents required) offers 354 sites ($16-29 daily) in four campgrounds, as well as three rustic mini-cabins; call 800/447-2757 or visit www.michigan.gov/dnr for reservations. The **Mason County Campground** (5906 W. Chauvez Rd., Ludington, 231/845-7609, $35 daily) has 50 modern sites and a wooded picnic area set among tall trees. A paved path leads visitors to Vista Point, a scenic overlook above Lake Michigan.

FOOD

While in Manistee, stop by the **Boathouse Grill** (440 River St., 231/723-2300, 11am-11pm Thurs.-Sat., 11am-10pm Sun.-Wed., $7-18), which serves comfort foods like chicken pot pie or crispy pan-fried lake perch. If the weather is nice, try to get a table on the patio overlooking the Manistee River. In Ludington, the **Jamesport Brewing Company** (410 S. James St., 231/845-2522, www.jamesportbrewingcompany.com, 11:30am-9pm Sun.-Thurs., 11:30am-10pm Fri.-Sat., $6-24) offers a wide array of salads, burgers, and other bar favorites, along with handcrafted beers.

INFORMATION AND SERVICES

For more information about this area, contact the **Manistee Convention & Visitors Bureau** (www.visitmanisteecounty.com), the **Manistee Area Chamber of Commerce** (11 Cypress St., Manistee, 800/288-2286, www.manisteechamber.com), the **Ludington Area Convention and Visitors Bureau** (5300 W. US-10, Ludington, 800/542-4600, www.pureludington.com), the **Pentwater Chamber of Commerce** (231/869-4150, www.pentwater.

org), the **Hart-Silver Lake/Mears Chamber & Visitors Bureau** (2388 N. Comfort Dr., Hart, 231/873-2247, www.thinkdunes.com), the **Newaygo County Convention & Visitors Bureau** (4686 S. Evergreen, Newaygo, 231/652-9298, www.newaygocountytourism.com), the **Mecosta County Area Convention & Visitors Bureau** (246 N. State, Big Rapids, 231/796-7640, www.bigrapids.org), and the **Cadillac Area Visitors Bureau** (222 Lake St., Cadillac, 231/775-0657, www.cadillacmichigan.com).

The towns along this route offer a limited number of services. For a bit more, head north to Traverse City, which offers everything from groceries to banks. If an emergency occurs, don't hesitate to dial **911** from any phone or visit **Mercy Hospital Cadillac** (400 Hobart St., 231/876-7200, www.munsonhealthcare.org).

GETTING THERE AND AROUND

To reach the towns and counties south of Traverse City, you can fly into **Cherry Capital Airport** (TVC, 727 Fly Don't Dr., Traverse City, 231/947-2250, www.tvcairport.com) or come by bus via **Greyhound** (231/946-5180 or 800/231-2222, www.greyhound.com) or **Indian Trails** (800/292-3831, www.indiantrails.com), after which you can rent a car and simply head south. From Traverse City, you can reach Manistee, Ludington, and the Pentwater area via US-31, cut through the Manistee National Forest on M-20, and drive north to Cadillac via US-131. Of course, it's also possible to reach the towns of Cadillac and Big Rapids (which lies about 42 miles south of Cadillac via US-131) directly by bus, courtesy of both Greyhound and Indian Trails.

Most travelers, however, will probably venture to this region via car, and luckily, there are plenty of helpful routes available. From Muskegon, for instance, you can access Pentwater, Ludington, and Manistee via US-31 North; without traffic, the 45-mile journey to Pentwater will usually take about 47 minutes, while the 59-mile trip to Ludington and the 83-mile trip to Manistee will take about 60 minutes and 80 minutes, respectively. From

Petoskey, meanwhile, you can access Cadillac via US-131 South, a 91-mile trip that usually takes less than two hours.

Lake Michigan Carferry

Ludington is also home to the Great Lakes' only authentic passenger steamship, offering two round-trip sailings each day in summer between Ludington and Manitowoc, Wisconsin. This historic carferry, the 410-foot-long SS *Badger* (701 Maritime Dr., Ludington, 920/684-0888 or 800/841-4243, www.ssbadger.com, round-trip $121 adults, $109 seniors 65 and over, $39 children 5-15, one-way $69 adults, $62 seniors 65 and over, $24 children 5-15, $86 pickup campers, $69 cars, vans, and pickups, $38 motorcycles, $6 bikes, children under 5 free), is the sole survivor of the fleet of auto/train/passenger ferries that once plowed across Lake Michigan, linking Midwestern cities like Chicago, Muskegon, and Milwaukee. The first steamer, the *Pere Marquette*, was hailed as a "titan of size and power." These hard-working vessels were owned by the railroads, and were even equipped with rails in their holds, so they could load boxcars as well as automobiles and passengers. The *Badger* operates daily mid-May-mid-October, though reservations are strongly recommended. Note, too, that pets must remain in your vehicle or in a ventilated kennel (which you must provide) on the car deck—a practice that's not recommended during the hot summer months. Also bear in mind that, for security reasons, you cannot access your vehicle during the crossing.

Charlevoix and Vicinity

Woodland Indians were likely the first to settle in present-day Charlevoix (SHAR-luh-voy), summering along the Lake Michigan shores some 4,000 years ago. But it was a French missionary who gave the town its name. Pierre François-Xavier de Charlevoix traveled through the region in the early 1700s, surreptitiously searching for the fabled Northwest Passage without tipping off the British. He never found a passage, of course, but that hasn't stopped boats from gathering in this yachter's paradise.

Nestled between Grand Traverse Bay and Little Traverse Bay, Charlevoix was practically destined to become a vacation spot. Along with the inherent appeal of Lake Michigan, Charlevoix also sidles up against lovely Lake Charlevoix, a clear, wishbone-shaped lake that draws anglers and pleasure boaters.

Inland, along the north arm of Lake Charlevoix toward Horton Bay, the land crumples like a fallen soufflé. This is lake country, river country, trout-fishing country, the boyhood backyard of a young Ernest Hemingway, whose family spent summers on nearby Walloon Lake. Just a few miles from the summer throngs that can descend on Charlevoix, much of Charlevoix County ticks along at a much mellower pace, the kind of place that inspires you to drift downstream in a canoe, make a few casts from a quiet bank, or pedal the two-lanes that twist through the region.

Or really get away from it all on Beaver Island, which you can reach by ferry or plane from Charlevoix. Originally settled by the Irish, it became a Mormon stronghold in the 1840s, ruled by a self-proclaimed king who was eventually assassinated by two of his followers. Things are considerably tamer on the island today, a sandy, wooded retreat with an Irish flavor and a decidedly somnolent air. Like much of the region, it's just the kind of place to spark creativity, maybe even inspire prose. Hey, it worked for Hemingway.

SIGHTS
Downtown

"Charlevoix the Beautiful," they call this nautical town of 3,000, wedged on an isthmus between Lake Michigan and Round Lake, which

© CHARLEVOIX AREA CVB

the Charlevoix harbor at night

opens to large Lake Charlevoix. With flowers flanking Bridge Street (US-31), a walkway along the Pine River linking the lakes, gleaming yachts with clanging halyards, screeching gulls, and yacht shops, Charlevoix *is* pretty beautiful.

Downtown Charlevoix also can be crammed on a summer weekend, so do yourself a favor: If you don't arrive by boat (as many do), leave the car at your hotel or on the edge of town and walk. This is a town meant for strolling, and you can enjoy nearly all of its sights on foot.

Bridge Street is Charlevoix's main drag, lined with restaurants, galleries, gift shops, and 50,000 petunias (planted by volunteers each spring, and watered by volunteers with a donated tank truck). For a free directory, stop by the **Charlevoix Area Convention & Visitors Bureau** (109 Mason St., 231/547-2101 or 800/367-8557, www.visitcharlevoix.com).

Toward the north end of the shopping district, a lift bridge rises on the half hour to allow tall-masted boats to travel the **Pine River Channel** from Lake Michigan to Round

Lake, essentially a yacht basin that connects to much larger Lake Charlevoix. A lovely walkway lit with Victorian-style lamps lines both sides of the channel between Bridge Street and Lake Michigan. Follow the north side to reach the long pier that extends far out into Lake Michigan. To your right, Michigan Avenue parallels the lakeshore, where stately old homes preside over the waterfront.

Follow the south side of the walkway to the **South Pierhead Lighthouse** and **Lake Michigan Beach,** with fine white sand, changing rooms, a playground, and a picnic area. The woods behind the beach have some short walking trails. Cross the street that parallels the beach, Park Avenue, to check out the weird elfin architecture of **Earl Young** scattered throughout this pleasant neighborhood. Young, a local real estate agent and self-taught home designer, constructed or remodeled two dozen homes in the 1930s and 1940s, many in the triangular block bordered by Park, Clinton, and Grant. Young used natural materials like enormous lake boulders to build his odd mushroom-shaped homes, topping them with curved cedar shake roofs. They're tucked amid Victorians, and it looks like Smurfs have invaded the neighborhood.

Young was also selected to design the Weathervane Terrace Inn and Stafford's Weathervane Restaurant along the channel. Rock walls and massive fireplaces characterize the designs; the restaurant's fireplace features a nine-ton keystone shaped like the state of Michigan. The local convention and visitors bureau has a map that directs you to Charlevoix's Young homes.

On the east side of Bridge Street, **East Park** fronts the bustling marina and city docks on Round Lake. This is a fun spot to grab a sandwich and watch the comings and goings of all the boat business. Even better, pick up some smoked fish from **John Cross Fisheries** (209 Belvedere Ave., 231/547-2532, 9am-5pm Mon.-Sat., 9am-4pm Sun.). One of the last commercial fisheries left in the area, it sells fresh walleye, perch, lake trout, and whitefish, which it also supplies to local restaurants. You can also buy smoked whitefish or trout by the chunk.

Northern Charlevoix

Around the southern end of Round Lake, the grounds of the century-old **Belvedere Club** spread across a high hill, overlooking both Round Lake and Lake Charlevoix. Founded by Baptists from Kalamazoo in the 1870s, the Belvedere Club was planned as a summer resort community, mirroring the Methodists' successful Bay View near Petoskey. Wealthy summer folk built homes in the opulent fashion of the day, with verandas, dormers, and gabled roofs. Today, many of the homes are occupied in summer by the grandchildren and great-grandchildren of the original owners. Though the streets through still-private Belvedere are closed in July and August, you can get a glimpse of the neighborhood from Ferry Avenue along Lake Charlevoix.

Inspired by the Belvedere Club, the First Congregational Church of Chicago formed a similar community on the north side of the Pine River Channel. As with the Belvedere, the

Chicago Club is closed to the public. Check out its fancy Victorians from East Dixon Avenue. As a bonus, this road also leads you to **Depot Beach,** a popular swimming beach, playground, and picnic area on Lake Charlevoix.

North of the city pier is Mt. McSauba Recreation Area, a municipal ski facility. At its northern end, Mt. McSauba shares a boundary with the **North Point Nature Preserve** (Mt. McSauba Rd. and Pleasant St., 231/347-0991, www.landtrust.org). The 27-acre preserve was purchased with funds raised by the people of Charlevoix, with help from the Michigan Natural Resources Trust Fund. Today, it offers several steep nature trails through hardwood forest and a pretty stretch of fairly secluded sand, home to threatened plant species like Pitcher's thistle. To reach the preserve, take US-31 north to Mercer Road, turn left onto Mt. McSauba Road, and turn right before the dirt road. The preserve will be on your left. For more information, contact the **Little Traverse Conservancy** (3264 Powell Rd., Harbor Springs, 231/347-0991, www.landtrust.org).

CHARLEVOIX VENETIAN FESTIVAL

Like several other communities along the Lake Michigan coast, Charlevoix presents its own **Venetian Festival** (231/547-3872, www.venetianfestival.com, free) in summer. Begun in 1930 as a simple candlelight boat parade, Charlevoix's version has grown to be the highlight of the season. Usually occurring in late July, the weeklong Charlevoix Venetian Festival offers daily events, from live concerts to athletic competitions, within the town's waterfront parks, in Round Lake Harbor, and on Lake Charlevoix, attracting tens of thousands of visitors each year. The annual event culminates in a beautiful Venetian Boat Parade on Round Lake, followed by a terrific fireworks display.

SHOPPING

Charlevoix's quaint downtown district offers its share of equally quaint shops. For unique children's clothing, check out **Ga Ga For Kids**

(323 Bridge St., 231/547-1600, 9am-6pm daily). Another fine clothing store is just down the street at the **Claymore Shop** (411 Bridge St., 231/237-0400, 9am-6pm daily). Exuding a "shop around the corner" vibe, the **Round Lake Bookstore** (107 Mason St., 231/547-2699, 10am-7pm daily) offers a great sampling of works by regional authors.

RECREATION
Hiking and Biking
The **Little Traverse Wheelway** extends for approximately 29 miles from Charlevoix to Harbor Springs. The trail is ideal for hiking, jogging, bicycling, and in-line skating. Horses and snowmobiles, however, are not permitted. The trail begins at the intersection of Division and Mt. McSauba Roads on the north side of Charlevoix.

Boating
Situated between Lake Michigan and several other inland lakes, Charlevoix is truly a boater's paradise. In fact, the area has three principal centers for boating: the Jordan River, Lake Charlevoix, and, of course, Lake Michigan, which has several access sites along the coast. Boaters and canoeists can access the Jordan River in East Jordan, at Old State Road, Webster's Bridge, and Roger's Bridge. Lake Charlevoix, meanwhile, presents lovely swimming beaches and several access points for boaters and anglers. Pleasure cruisers can view several sights along the Lake Charlevoix shoreline, from some of the area's most beautiful homes to an old shipwreck at Oyster Bay.

Skiing
About a half mile north of the city pier lies the **Mt. McSauba Recreation Area** (231/547-3253), one of the state's few municipal ski facilities. Overlooking Lake Michigan, it lures downhill and cross-country skiers. Other popular wintertime activities include snowboarding, snowshoeing, sledding, and ice skating. The groomed 1.2-mile cross-country trail is even lit at night.

ACCOMMODATIONS AND FOOD
Accommodations
Charlevoix can get pretty busy, especially during the summer months, so make reservations early before coming into town. That said, Charlevoix has loads of lodging possibilities, from basic motels on US-31 to swanky condos along the waterfront.

The **Edgewater Inn** (100 Michigan Ave., 231/547-6044, www.edgewater-charlevoix. com, $89-389 d) has suites on Round Lake and amenities like an indoor/outdoor pool and full kitchen facilities. The **Weathervane Terrace Inn & Suites** (111 Pine River Ln., 231/547-9955, www.weathervane-chx.com, $59-299 d) sits directly on the channel, offering an outdoor pool and hot tub as well as views of Lake Michigan and Round Lake. The **Charlevoix Inn & Suites** (800 Petoskey Ave., 231/547-0300, www.charlevoixinnandsuites. com, $50-150 d) offers less expensive accommodations, with an indoor pool and proximity to Lake Charlevoix beaches.

Food
The **Stafford's Weathervane Restaurant** (106 Pine River Ln., 231/547-4311, www.staffords.com, 11am-8:30pm Sun.-Thurs., 11am-9:30pm Fri.-Sat., $10-25) is one of Charlevoix's best restaurants, in terms of both food and location. Affiliated with the Stafford restaurants of Petoskey, it specializes in planked whitefish and steaks, and overlooks the Pine River Channel. Outside seating is available for lunch and dinner. **Terry's** (101 Antrim St., 231/547-2799, www.terrysofcharlevoix.com, 5pm-close daily, $23-36) is frequented for its fresh walleye and whitefish.

INFORMATION AND SERVICES
Information
For more information about the Charlevoix area, contact the **Charlevoix Area Chamber of Commerce** (109 Mason St., 231/547-2101, www.charlevoix.org, 9am-5pm Mon.-Fri.), the **Charlevoix Area Convention & Visitors**

Stafford's Weathervane Restaurant in Charlevoix

Bureau (109 Mason St., 231/547-2101 or 800/367-8557, www.visitcharlevoix.com), or the **Petoskey Area Visitors Bureau** (401 E. Mitchell St., 231/348-2755, www.boynecountry.com, 8am-4pm Mon.-Fri.). For local news and events, consult the *Charlevoix Courier* (www.charlevoixcourier.com).

Services

Charlevoix may be a small town, but it still has its share of necessary services, such as beauty salons, pharmacies, and banks. There are even several **post offices** in the area, including one near downtown Charlevoix (6700 M-66 N., 231/547-2631, www.usps.com). For medical services, consult the **Charlevoix Area Hospital** (14700 Lakeshore Dr., 231/547-4024, www.cah.org). If an emergency occurs, don't hesitate to call **911** from any phone.

GETTING THERE AND AROUND

Travelers can access Charlevoix in a variety of ways. One option is to fly into **Cherry Capital**

Airport (TVC, 727 Fly Don't Dr., Traverse City, 231/947-2250, www.tvcairport.com) or **Pellston Regional Airport** (PLN, 1395 US-31, Pellston, 231/539-8441 or 231/539-8442, www.pellstonairport.com), rent a vehicle, and take US-31 to Charlevoix. From the Traverse City airport, you'll take CR-620, 3 Mile Road, and US-31 North to reach Charlevoix; without traffic, the 48-mile trip usually takes about 55 minutes. From the Pellston airport, meanwhile, you'll take US-31 South along the coast to Charlevoix; without traffic, the 36-mile trip should take about 47 minutes. Another possibility is to arrive via bus; after all, both **Greyhound** (800/231-2222, www.greyhound.com) and **Indian Trails** (800/292-3831, www.indiantrails.com) provide service to the **Beaver Island Boat Company** (103 Bridge Park Dr., 888/446-4095, www.bibco.com) in downtown Charlevoix. With several marinas in the area, it's also possible to arrive in Charlevoix by boat.

Of course, most visitors come via car, which is an ideal way to explore the surrounding towns and lakes. From Sault Ste. Marie, for instance, you'll take I-75 South, cross the Mackinac Bridge (a toll bridge), and merge onto US-31 South to reach Charlevoix, a 110-mile trip that normally takes about 2 hours. From downtown Detroit, meanwhile, you can follow I-375 North to I-75 North, take M-32 West and various surface streets to M-66 North, and continue to US-31 North; without traffic, the 274-mile trip will require about 4.25 hours. No matter how you reach Charlevoix, though, you can easily get around town via car, bike, or foot. In addition, some travelers choose to rely on the **Charlevoix Cab Co.** (231/547-9700, www. charlevoixcab.com), which offers 24-hour service around Charlevoix County.

FISHERMAN'S ISLAND STATE PARK

Five miles south of Charlevoix off US-31, **Fisherman's Island State Park** (16480 Bells Bay Rd., 231/547-6641, annual $11 Recreation Passport for Michigan residents or $8.40 day-use fee/$30.50 yearly Recreation Passport for nonresidents required) does indeed encompass a little 10-acre offshore island, but most visitors come to enjoy its five miles of lakeshore and wooded dunes. With long stretches of soft sand and exceptionally clear water, it's a particularly good spot to hunt for Petoskey stones.

There's evidence that Woodland Indians inhabited Fisherman's Island more than 1,000 years ago. In the early 1900s, one enterprising Charlevoix innkeeper planned a casino for the site. But those plans died with the property owner, and the state eventually acquired the island and nearby shoreline, naming it a state park in 1978. Today, the small island is inhabited only by birds and insects. Wading or swimming to it is not recommended, since a strong current often rushes between the island and mainland.

The park is nearly divided in two by a parcel of private property in its middle. The northern portion is the more popular of the two state park sections, with five miles of hiking trails, a pretty day-use area, and 81 rustic campsites. Most are nice, private sites in the woods near

the water; if you're really lucky, you'll snag one of the dozen or so sites right on the beach.

To reach the day-use area, hike the marked trail along the dune ridge, or drive south on the park road past the campgrounds. It has grills, picnic tables, outhouses, and a trail leading across bubbling Inwood Creek to the beach. On a clear day, you can see the tip of the Leelanau Peninsula from this fine stretch of beach, and you'll often be treated to a spectacular sunset. For real solitude, access the southern end of the park from the town of Norwood, 11 miles south on US-31. Follow signs to Norwood Township Park on the shoreline, then trace the double track into the state park. (Driving is not recommended if it's wet.) You're likely to have the beach and old truck trails all to yourself.

LAKE CHARLEVOIX
Horton Bay

Several authors and artists have roots in northern Michigan, but none as celebrated as Ernest Hemingway. Hemingway spent his childhood summers at the family cottage on nearby Walloon Lake, fished the waters of Lake Charlevoix, hunted on the point at Horton Bay, and once escaped a game warden by fleeing across the lake's north arm to the point between the arms, now known as Hemingway Point.

The tiny town of Horton Bay, on Boyne City Road about 10 miles east of Charlevoix, played a special role in Hemingway's life. He whiled away summer afternoons on the front steps of the classic false-front, white-clapboard general store, which he describes in his short story "Up in Michigan." (He drew on many of his surroundings, in fact, for his Nick Adams short stories.) Later, he married his first wife, Hadley Richardson, at Horton Bay's Congregational Church.

Today, the **Horton Bay General Store** (5115 Boyne City Rd., 231/582-7827, www.hortonbaygeneralstore.com, 8am-5pm daily, $9-18) is preserved more as a shrine to Hemingway than a store and eatery—light on foodstuffs but heavy on Hemingway nostalgia. Built in 1876, the cavernous building is filled with Hemingway photos, novels, even a copy of his

1922 marriage certificate. There's a small lunch counter and a few assorted groceries. But it's the charming old building itself that draws you in. Steeped in literary history, its inviting front porch is still a great place to while away a summer afternoon.

Boyne City

At the foot of Lake Charlevoix, pleasant and relaxing Boyne City was once a loud industrial town. In the 19th century, Boyne City thrived as a regional logging center, with 90 miles of railroad track and several hundred logging cars linking the town to the surrounding logging camps and feeding its hungry sawmills. Tanneries also became big business at the turn of the 20th century, using bark from the hemlock tree to tan leather. One Boyne City tannery produced six million pounds of shoe leather annually.

Boyne City has done a fine job preserving some of its historic buildings, with a main street that looks like it could be in the Wild West. The best example is the **Wolverine-Dilworth Inn** (300 Water St.), a 1911 landmark and former hotel, boasting a spacious veranda, a terrazzo tile lobby with fireplace, and a saloon-style dining room.

Boyne Mountain

Six miles southeast of Boyne City in Boyne Falls, Everett Kircher carved out his own piece of history at Boyne Mountain (1 Boyne Mountain Rd., Boyne Falls, 231/549-6000 or 800/462-6963, www.boyne.com). A Studebaker dealer from the Detroit area, Kircher figured out that Detroit's booming auto industry would make for a lot of wealthy Michigan residents, many of whom would be looking for a place to vacation. He obtained some farmland near Boyne Falls and proceeded to develop the area's first downhill ski resort. Boyne Mountain opened in 1947.

Over the years, the visionary Kircher became known for "firsts"—the Midwest's first chairlift in 1948, the nation's first freestyle skiing exhibition in 1961, the world's first quad chairlift in 1967, the state's first high-speed quad in

1990, and the nation's first six-person chair in 1992. Kircher was the first to perfect artificial snowmaking, and Boyne's patented snowguns are used at resorts all over the world. Olympic ski planners still contact Boyne for snowmaking consultation.

Even in his 80s, Everett Kircher would come to Boyne headquarters in Boyne Falls nearly every day, overseeing a privately held ski/golf enterprise that seems to grow exponentially every year. In the tightly consolidated ski industry, Boyne is a player: It owns three impressive ski resorts in Michigan. The company's not doing too badly in the golf industry department either, with its spectacular Bay Harbor development near Petoskey.

By those standards, Boyne Mountain seems almost quaint, but it is an extremely popular resort in summer and winter. The ski area offers over 40 runs, including the Disciples Ridge area, which features some of the steepest pitches in the state. The property also has over 20 miles of groomed and tracked trails for cross-country skiing, which double as mountain biking trails. Come summer, two 18-hole golf courses help fill Boyne Mountain's 600-plus rooms (and its jumbo 30-person outdoor hot tub).

Jordan River

You'll better understand Ernest Hemingway's love for this land after passing a little time along the Jordan River, which empties into Lake Charlevoix's south arm. Look for the small wooden canoe signs that signify access points, like the one along Alba Road near the Charlevoix-Antrim county line. Here, the Jordan rolls silently northward, the pale brown of hospital coffee, framed by weeping willows and grassy banks. Though anglers hate to advertise it, the Jordan is one of the finest trout streams in the state.

The Jordan River valley cuts a wide swath through the landscape south of Lake Charlevoix, and nowhere is the view more dramatic than from **Dead Man's Hill,** off US-131 south of Boyne Falls. Two miles south of M-32 West, watch for Dead Man's Hill Road; turn west and travel 1.5 miles or so to the end. Here, the flat country lane suddenly falls away to reveal a marvelous valley more than 1,000 feet below: The Jordan straggles through a woodland of pines interspersed with beech and maple, reaching out across the lowlands like spider veins.

The morbid name is in reference to Stanley Graczyk, a 21-year-old logger who, in 1910, mistakenly drove his team of horses up the hill and right over the edge. Whoops. Dead Man's Hill is also the trailhead for the **Jordan River Pathway,** which loops 18 miles through the valley floor. There's a marked 3-mile loop, too. Maps are available at the trailhead.

Ironton Ferry

Up M-66, the tiny **Ironton Ferry** (6:30am-10pm daily, $3.25 vehicles, $0.50 pedestrians) chugs its way from Ironton across the narrows of Lake Charlevoix's south arm to Hemingway Point—a distance of about 100 yards. The U.S. flag flies gallantly from the *Charlevoix's* white steel pilothouse; a sign sternly warns auto passengers—all three of them—that "We will not be responsible for vehicles left unattended"—a difficult task, considering you can't even open the car door wide enough to get out. The funky little ferry even made the "Ripley's Believe It or Not" newspaper feature, noting that its captain traveled more than 15,000 miles without ever being more than 1,000 feet from home.

It is efficient. The *Charlevoix* takes just two minutes to follow its cable to the far shore, and just a little over four minutes to unload, reload, and be back again—but saves a 15-mile trip around the south arm of the lake. People have found it to be a worthwhile service since 1876. Its "1884 Rates for Ferriage" are still posted: "Double Teams, 0.30; Single Teams, 0.20; Beast, 0.10 except sheep; Sheep, 0.10 up to 6, 0.05 over 6; footmen, 0.05 without beast."

ELLSWORTH AND VICINITY

Eleven miles south of Charlevoix on CR-65, Ellsworth wouldn't be much more than a wide spot in the road but for a couple of very notable exceptions: The Rowe Inn Restaurant and Tapawingo. These two restaurants have put unlikely Ellsworth on the map, with rave reviews in national publications like *Gourmet* and *Wine Spectator.* Unfortunately, a poor economic climate forced Tapawingo to close its doors in 2009, but happily, **The Rowe Inn** (6303 E. Jordan Rd., 231/588-7351 or 866/432-5873, www.roweinn.com, 5pm-close Mon.-Sat., noon-2pm and 5pm-close Sun., $20-39) remains. With a rather rustic decor and one-of-a-kind entrées like duck magret with port-cinnamon sauce, The Rowe has attracted quite a following. Its distinctive menu—thick with rich local ingredients like duck, veal, trout, morels, and fresh berries—and the largest and most outstanding wine cellar in Michigan have earned it a spot among the nation's top restaurants.

Shanty Creek

If you're looking for a year-round destination that accommodates a yen for golf, hiking, biking, winter sports, and much more, consider visiting **Shanty Creek Resorts** (1 Shanty Creek Rd., Bellaire, 800/678-4111, www.shantycreek.com), a half-hour's drive south of Charlevoix. Separated into three villages—Cedar River, Schuss, and Summit—this enormous 4,500-acre swath of land features several dining, lodging, and spa options, three award-winning golf courses, numerous downhill skiing runs, and a fantastic trail network for cross-country skiers and mountain bikers.

The main draw here is golfing ($18-108 pp), which is usually available April-October, weather depending. Summit Village, which offers a newly renovated hotel and conference center, also presents two favored courses: **The Legend,** designed by Arnold Palmer and named the best course in the Midwest by readers of *Golf Magazine,* and the more wide-open **Summit Golf Course,** the resort's original course. In addition, Summit Village boasts heated indoor and outdoor pools, a spa and fitness center, and a downhill ski area with a dozen slopes.

Five minutes away, Schuss Mountain offers more advanced skiing, with 37 runs, three terrain parks, and seven lifts. Its Bavarian-style base area is smaller, with a scattering of villas and condos. This village also has its share of other diversions, including the challenging **Schuss Mountain Golf Course,** set amid abundant wetlands and rolling hills.

The newest resort, Cedar River Village, houses 14 condos, over 70 luxurious suites, two restaurants, and **Cedar River Golf Course,** situated amid verdant hills and peaceful waters. Between the three resorts, over 13 miles of groomed and tracked cross-country trails wind through hilly terrain and hardwood forest. In summer, many of those same trails become prime mountain biking terrain. The network includes beginner to expert trails, some made even more difficult by the area's sandy terrain.

BEAVER ISLAND

Traveling to Beaver Island is kind of slow, rather expensive, and there isn't much to do when you get there. There is no must-see

attraction and no particularly spectacular scenery on this flat, wooded island. Nope, Beaver Island ticks along at a rather sleepy, predictable pace: The bank opens every Tuesday 9am-1pm. The ferry brings the mail. When Island Airways arrives from Charlevoix, everybody leaving pretty much knows everybody arriving.

If this sounds hopelessly dull, then don't go to Beaver Island. There is precious little in the way of formal entertainment on Beaver, save for some occasional Irish music and beer drinking at the Shamrock Bar. Though it ranks as the largest island in Michigan—13 miles long and 6 miles wide—you won't find any towns outside the port of St. James, just simple cottages and 100 miles of sandy roads.

On the other hand, if the inherent isolation and somnolent pace appeal to you, then by all means, go. Stranded 18 miles from the nearest Lower Peninsula shoreline, Beaver Island is the most remote inhabited island in the Great

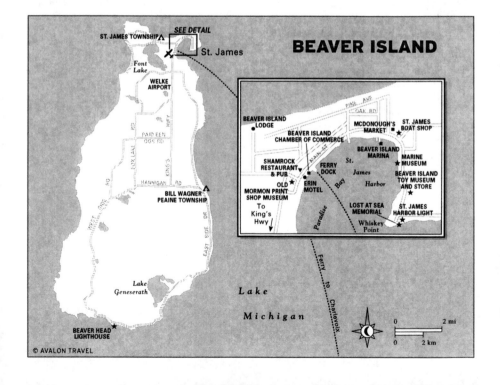

Lakes, offering what may be a quintessential glimpse of island life: unhurried, unbothered, unaffected by whim and fashion. You make your own entertainment here, and it can be delightful. Bike a quiet road to an even quieter beach. Explore the island's quirky history at a couple of terrific little museums. Buy a local a cup of coffee and talk island politics. Paddle a kayak to another island in the Beaver archipelago. Take off your watch.

Sights

Beaver Island activity centers around St. James on hook-shaped Beaver Harbor, which many locals still call by its 19th-century name, Paradise Bay. This is where the ferry lands, and where you'll find the sum of the island's commercial development. Everything in St. James is within walking distance.

You can pick up much of the island's colorful history and character without ever leaving the harbor. The **Shamrock Restaurant & Pub** (26245 Main St., 231/448-2278, www.shamrockbarrestaurant.com, 11am-9pm daily, $12-19) is the most popular spot in town for a burger, beer, and island news. At the **St. James Boat Shop** (38230 Michigan, 231/448-2365, www.stjamesboatshop.com), Bill Freese builds gorgeous wood-strip canoes and kayaks, along with beautiful handmade wooden buckets.

From the boat shop, it's just a short walk to Whiskey Point, the **Lost at Sea memorial,** and the **St. James Harbor Light,** marking the entrance to this well-protected natural harbor. The 19th-century light was "manned" for years by Beaver Island native Elizabeth Whitney Williams, the only woman light keeper on the Great Lakes.

The southern half of the island has far more public land than the northern half, much of it a state wildlife research area. It has several small lakes, bogs, unimproved roads, and trails that are fun to explore, especially if you have a mountain bike. Fish in **Lake Geneserath,** swim at several sandy beaches on the southern shore, or check out the **Beaver Head Lighthouse** near the island's southern tip, a pretty cream-brick house and tower built in 1858, one of the oldest

on all the Great Lakes. Back in the 1920s, thrill-seekers from Charlevoix drove across the thick lake ice, headed for Beaver Island. When a thick fog left them completely disoriented, the keeper guided them to safety with the light's fog signal.

If you plan to explore Beaver Island on your own, pick up two maps in St. James first: the comprehensive island map available at **McDonough's Market** (38240 Michigan Ave., 231/448-2736, www.mcdonoughsmarket.com) and a small history map, available at the chamber of commerce. It points out several noteworthy attractions that you can seek out on your own.

Kayaking

Eleven other islands scatter around Beaver's northern half, an inviting archipelago for sea kayakers. The islands range in distance from Garden (2 miles away) to Gull (11 miles). Garden, practically due north from St. James, is probably the most intriguing for paddlers, with several protected bays and inlets. High Island, four miles west, has bluffs along the western shore rising to 240 feet. Most of High and Garden are public land, part of the **Beaver Islands State Wildlife Research Area.** Some of the smaller islands are privately owned or otherwise off-limits to preserve nesting sites. For more information, contact the **Gaylord DNR Operations Service Center** (Wildlife Office, 1732 W. M-32, Gaylord, 989/732-3541, www.michigan.gov/dnr).

The **Inland Seas School of Kayaking** (231/448-2221, www.inlandseaskayaking.com) offers instruction and guided tours. If you plan to do any inter-island paddling, observe all the usual safety precautions, watch the weather, and make sure you have a good nautical chart. The open waters of the Great Lakes are not for amateurs.

Accommodations

There are several motels, lodges, B&Bs, and cabins for rent on the island. Near the ferry dock, the **Erin Motel** (231/448-2240, $69-99 d) overlooks the water with a sand beach. The

Beaver Island Lodge (231/448-2396, www. beaverislandlodge.com, $120-190 d) sits along a secluded stretch of beach west of town, with nice rooms and an on-site restaurant.

The island has two rustic campgrounds (with pit toilets and water), both on the lakeshore. The **St. James Township Campground** is on the north side of the island one mile from town, and has 12 sites. The **Bill Wagner Peaine Township Campground,** with 22 sites, is along the east shore, seven miles south of town. Both are $10 per night (no reservations). There are two grocery stores and a handful of restaurants on the island.

Information and Services
For information about Beaver Island's services, businesses, and lodging options, contact the **Beaver Island Chamber of Commerce** (231/448-2505, www.beaverisland.org). For local news and events, consult the monthly *Beaver Beacon* (www.beaverisland.net).

Getting There and Around
Commercial transportation to Beaver Island is available only from Charlevoix, which lies about 32 miles away. The **Beaver Island Boat Company** (103 Bridge Park Dr., 231/547-2311 or 888/446-4095, www.bibco.com, one-way $24-29 adults, $12-17 children 5-14, children under 5 free, $25 canoes or kayaks, $10 bikes, rates vary for pets and vehicles) makes scheduled trips April-December, with two trips daily during most of the summer. It takes a little over two hours each way, and the 95-foot-long *Beaver Islander* or 130-foot-long *Emerald Isle* can be a bit of a rough ride in choppy waters. Reservations are recommended for passengers and required for autos. If you take the first ferry in the morning, you can make Beaver Island a day trip of six hours or so, returning on the late afternoon ferry. Of course, the time constraints will limit you to exploring just a small portion of the island.

Island Airways (111 Airport Dr., 800/524-6895, www.islandairways.com, one-way $47 adults, $44 seniors 65 and over, $33 children 2-9, children under 2 and small pets free, $23 large pets, $10 bikes), meanwhile, provides daily air service from Charlevoix in a little 10-seater. The flight takes about 20 minutes, and reservations are required.

In truth, it's probably not necessary to have a car on Beaver Island. Though the island is quite large and has more than 100 miles of roads, downtown St. James is ideal for walking and biking. In addition, many accommodations provide transportation from the dock or airport; if there's something specific you want to see (such as the lighthouse on the southern shore), you can usually rent a vehicle for about $55 daily from **Gordon's Auto Rentals and Clinic** (231/448-2438). Just remember to reserve ahead of time.

Petoskey and Vicinity

Petoskey (puh-TOS-kee) was originally settled by the Ottawa Indians in the 1700s and takes its name from a local Native American, Petosega. With bountiful fishing and hunting, the region was a desirable place to live, and Ottawa and Ojibwa tribes thrived here. In the 1800s, the federal government negotiated more equitably with local tribes than it did elsewhere in the young nation; tribes were given the first choice of land (albeit their land!) until 1875.

White settlers began arriving in the 1850s, establishing logging operations along the Bear River, the name the town used until 1873. With a sawmill, a lime quarry, and other enterprises along the river and Little Traverse Bay, Bear River quickly became an industrial town of buzzing saws and belching smoke.

But the town began changing with the arrival of the railroad in 1873. Lured north by the beautiful Lake Michigan waters and cool northern air, residents from southern Great Lakes cities like Chicago and Detroit began migrating to Petoskey, gradually converting its industrial squalor to an elegant summer getaway. The artesian springs that bubbled throughout town and their "health-giving waters" only encouraged Petoskey's growth.

By the turn of the 20th century, Petoskey's downtown was filled with fine shops and 13 grand resort hotels like the Arlington, with its imposing columns, dance hall, and 24-foot-wide veranda. At its heyday in 1900, three trains a day stopped at the Arlington, which could sleep 800—surpassed only by the rival Grand Hotel on Mackinac Island. Unfortunately, the Arlington burned to the ground in 1915, the same fate that met almost every single one of Petoskey's grand resorts— The Jewel, The Imperial, the City Hotel. Only the Perry Hotel, made of expensive brick, still stands.

Thankfully, plenty of other historic buildings still stand in the Petoskey area, a city that wisely realized early the value of protecting them. From its well-preserved Gaslight District to the entire Victorian neighborhood of Bay View, Petoskey maintains the charm of the grand resort era, along with the natural resources that brought summer visitors here in the first place. Equally appealing to anglers, boaters, shoppers, golfers, and skiers, the town has so far been able to balance its need for tourism with its desire for preservation, but only time and resolve will determine if it will last. In 1996, the National Trust for Historic Preservation listed Petoskey as one of 10 national historic treasures most worthy of fighting for, warning that "retail, roadway, and residential sprawl threaten the town's historic character and pastoral setting."

SIGHTS
Gaslight District

Though growth indeed threatens Petoskey— busy US-31 slices right between downtown and the waterfront—it remains a charming city for vacationers, with a downtown made for strolling. The Gaslight District anchors the downtown, an eight-block area of well-preserved Victorian brick storefronts filled with shops

Petoskey's historic Gaslight District

and restaurants that has drawn shoppers since the early 1900s. A low-interest loan program sponsored by the regional chamber of commerce encourages their preservation and renovation. Centered around Lake and Howard Streets, the district mixes high-brow boutiques with bookstores, art galleries, antiques haunts, and homegrown souvenir shops.

Crooked Tree Arts Center

If you enjoy strolling through art galleries, then you're in luck. Despite its relatively small size, Petoskey's Gaslight District boasts several worthy choices. One such option is the **Crooked Tree Arts Center** (CTAC, 461 E. Mitchell St., 231/347-4337, www.crookedtree.org, 9am-5pm Mon.-Tues. and Thurs.-Fri., 10am-5pm Wed., 10am-4pm Sat., free). Founded in 1971 as the Crooked Tree Arts Council, the CTAC was established for three reasons: to bring more culture to northern Michiganders, support local and regional artists, and form an umbrella organization that could provide cultural services to the people of both Charlevoix and Emmet

© LAURA MARTONE

the Crooked Tree Arts Center

Counties. Initially, the CTAC operated out of members' homes—that is, until 1978, when the old United Methodist Church in downtown Petoskey became available for purchase. Built in 1890, the church soon became the official home of the CTAC, and today, the multicolored building is hard to ignore. It's also hard to dismiss all the artistic and educational activities that take place inside, including dance and visual arts classes, wine-tasting events, live concerts, and theatrical performances. Of course, you're also welcome to wander through the on-site art galleries, which house rotating exhibits that feature the paintings, photographs, sculptures, and other creations of many Michigan-based artists. Recent exhibits, for instance, have showcased Robert deJonge's images of the state's scenic shorelines and a colorful collection of children's book illustrations, donated by Francis Molson, a retired English professor from Central Michigan University.

Of course, the CTAC isn't Petoskey's only attraction for art lovers. Only a few blocks to the north, you'll encounter **Stafford's Gallery of Art & History** (410 Rose St., 231/347-0142, www.staffords.com, 10am-6pm Mon.-Sat., 10am-4pm Sun., free), which is located behind the historic Stafford's Perry Hotel. Housed in an old warehouse building that was once a 1930s-era icehouse, a meat-packing company, an ice cream plant, and, from 1969 to 2007, Longton Hall Antiques, this spacious fine art gallery presents a wide assortment of watercolor and oil paintings, photographs, sculptures, jewelry, gifts, and original prints by nearly 40 Michigan artists. Recent offerings have included Valerie Thomson's impressionistic landscapes of northern Michigan locales; Michael McPeak's photographs, which are curiously printed on light-penetrating silk; John Riepma's colorful, hand-blown glass sculptures; Janet Lewandowski's whimsical, wool-based "steampunk" dolls; and Tera Jackson's dichroic glass rings, pendants, necklaces, and earrings. Here, you may also spot antiques as well as Stafford's exclusive collection of artifacts and photographs that represent the history of downtown Petoskey from the late

19th century to the early 20th century, with an emphasis on the nearly two dozen hotels that once dominated this area.

Little Traverse History Museum

Near the intersection of Petoskey and Bay Streets, follow the pedestrian tunnel under US-31 to **Bayfront Park,** which merges with **Sunset Park** to the east, offering a vast green space along the waterfront. Once the center of Petoskey's sawmill operations, now this beautifully renovated area comprises a marina, a walkway along the Bear River, one of the area's historic mineral springs, and the fine **Little Traverse History Museum** (231/347-2620, www.petoskeymuseum.org, 10am-4pm Mon.-Sat. Memorial Day-mid-Oct., $3 adults, children under 11 free) in the restored rail depot.

The museum is crammed full of interesting displays, including a photo collection of Petoskey's old hotels and an exhibit detailing the sad tale of the passenger pigeon, which migrated to the Little Traverse Bay area by the billions (yes, *billions*) in the 1870s. Accounts tell of the skies blackening when the birds were in flight, with individual flocks stretching for miles and miles. Alas, the nesting habits and docile nature of the pigeons made them easy to hunt by simply clubbing them to death in their nests. Entrepreneurs did so with glee, since their meat was considered a delicacy. By the 1870s, entire steamships were loaded with pigeons for delivery to urban restaurants in the southern Great Lakes. In less than 25 years, the passenger pigeon had completely disappeared from the region; by 1914, it became officially extinct.

Probably the museum's most popular display is the collection of Ernest Hemingway memorabilia. Hemingway's family began vacationing on nearby Walloon Lake when Hemingway was just a boy, and the family still owns a couple of acres of land there. After he was injured in World War I, Hemingway recuperated in Petoskey, living in a rooming house at the corner of State and Woodland Streets in 1919-1920. Here, he gathered material and began drafting *Torrents of Spring,* which alludes to several Petoskey locations. The museum's display includes first editions of that classic novel as well as *For Whom the Bell Tolls* and *A Farewell to Arms.*

Hemingway overshadows Petoskey's other famous author, Bruce Catton, who won a Pulitzer Prize in 1954 for his Civil War account *A Stillness at Appomattox.* The Little Traverse History Museum gives him his due.

Near the museum, you can pick up the **Top of Michigan trail,** a 15-mile paved, off-road path that stretches from Bay Harbor through Petoskey to Harbor Springs. Several other trails radiate off this route, creating a network of 180 miles of multiuse recreation pathways between Charlevoix and Mackinaw City. Trail maps are available at the Petoskey Area Visitors Bureau.

ENTERTAINMENT

Just outside town, the **Odawa Casino Resort** (1760 Lears Rd., 877/442-6464, www.odawacasino.com, 24 hours daily) provides a 300,000-square-foot entertainment complex, with gaming, restaurants, and a theater that books big-name talent on a regular basis. They also have O zone, a state-of-the-art nightclub that compares to many of the hot spots in Vegas.

SHOPPING

Petoskey's delightful Gaslight District offers a wide assortment of shops. **American Spoon** (411 E. Lake St., 231/347-1738, www.spoon.com, 9am-7pm daily) offers an assortment of delicious jams, sauces, and more, all made from local produce and other fresh ingredients. Check out the adjacent café for delicious sandwiches made with their sauces. **McLean & Eakin Booksellers** (307 E. Lake St., 231/347-1180, www.mcleanandeakin.com, 9am-8pm Mon.-Sat., 10am-5pm Sun.) offers an eclectic assortment of titles and regularly hosts educational and literary events. If antiques are more your style, stop in at **Longton Hall Antiques** (329 Bay St., 231/347-9672, www.longtonhallantiques.com, 9am-7pm Mon.-Sat., 11am-5pm Sun.).

© DANIEL MARTONE

locally made condiments at American Spoon

SPORTS AND RECREATION
Golf

While the area around Traverse City and Charlevoix boasts several terrific courses, the Petoskey/Harbor Springs area has no shortage of great golf either. Several lodgings even offer packages and will reserve tee times.

Best known are the four courses at **Boyne Highlands Resort** (600 Highland Dr., 231/526-3000 or 800/462-6963, www.boyne. com, daily May-Oct., $40-145 pp), a ski/golf resort a few miles north of Harbor Springs: The Moor, the Donald Ross Memorial, The Heather, and the Arthur Hills. *Golf Magazine* considers The Heather course, designed by Robert Trent Jones, one of the top courses in the country, with lots of sculpted bunkers and water hazards (and cool global positioning systems on the carts to feed you yardage information). The Ross Memorial course is a perennial favorite. It re-creates several of the most famous holes throughout the world designed by Ross, considered by many to be the "father of golf course architecture."

Boyne also operates the **Crooked Tree Golf Club** (Bay Harbor, 231/439-4030 or 800/462-6963, www.boyne.com, $35-65 pp), a British-style course overlooking Little Traverse Bay near Petoskey. In Harbor Springs, the **Harbor Point Golf Course** (8475 S. Lake Shore Dr., 231/526-2951, www.harborpointgolfclub.com, $55 pp w/cart) had been an exclusive private club since 1896; it's now open to the public in the spring and fall months and considered a favorite walking course by *Golf Digest*.

Near Burt Lake in Brutus, **Hidden River Golf & Casting Club** (7688 Maple River Rd., 231/529-4653, www.hiddenriver.com, daily Apr.-Oct., $40-91 pp) offers classic "up north" scenery, with tall stands of pine and hardwoods and the meandering Maple River; this resort is also popular for fly-fishing.

Winter Activities

Nub's Nob (500 Nubs Nob Rd., Harbor Springs, 231/526-2131, www.nubsnob.com, lift tickets $41-69 pp) often gets overshadowed by the Boynes, but it has its own loyal following.

The well-protected, wooded slopes (blocked from cold winter winds) are best known for short and steep faces like Twilight Zone and Scarface, but its 23 trails and 427-foot vertical drop have plenty of beginner and intermediate terrain, too. If Boyne Highlands gets crowded, this is the place to escape.

ACCOMMODATIONS AND FOOD
Accommodations
Petoskey offers an enormous array of lodgings, from basic motels along US-31 to resort complexes to condo units that are especially convenient for families or groups.

Unless you're on a tight budget, opt for a stay at the lemon chiffon-colored **((Stafford's Perry Hotel** (100 Lewis St., 231/347-4000, www.staffords.com, $99-319 d), which overlooks Little Traverse Bay and dates back to 1899. Today, it's run by successful local innkeeper/restaurateur Stafford Smith, who has done a wonderful job of updating the venerable old building while retaining every bit of its

charm. Rates are reasonable for such a treasure. The Perry also features three separate dining choices, if you just want to relax and don't feel like wandering around town.

The **Terrace Inn** (1549 Glendale, 800/530-9898, www.theterraceinn.com, $79-189 d) provides an elegant bed-and-breakfast experience in a turn-of-the-20th-century building. If you're on a tighter budget, try the **Econo Lodge South** (1859 US-131 S, 231/348-3324, www.econolodge.com, $59-150 d).

Food
Petoskey also offers a superb array of dining options, especially in the downtown area. Since 1875, the historic **City Park Grill** (432 E. Lake St., 231/347-0101, www.cityparkgrill.com, 11:30am-9pm Mon.-Thurs. and Sun., 11:30am-10pm Fri.-Sat., extended bar hours, $7-24) has lured residents and visitors alike, despite several transformations over the years. Today, patrons come for the happy-hour specials and live weekend music in the adjacent bar, plus an eclectic restaurant menu that includes shellfish

© LAURA MARTONE

Stafford's Perry Hotel in Petoskey

chowder, jambalaya, almond-crusted whitefish, and filet mignon with blue cheese sauce.

Another delectable downtown eatery is **Grand Traverse Pie Company** (316 E. Mitchell St., 231/348-4060, www.gtpie.com, 7am-6:30pm Mon.-Sat., $4-13), part of a statewide chain that offers scrumptious soups, salads, sandwiches, quiches, and, naturally, pies—from the Suttons Bay Blueberry to the Glen Haven Peach Crumb.

INFORMATION AND SERVICES
Information
For more information about the Petoskey area, contact the **Petoskey Area Visitors Bureau** (401 E. Mitchell St., 231/348-2755, www.boynecountry.com, 8am-4pm Mon.-Fri.) or the **Petoskey Regional Chamber of Commerce** (401 E. Mitchell St., 231/347-4150, www.petoskey.com). For local news and events, consult the *Petoskey News-Review* (www.petoskeynews.com).

Services
Though a relatively small town, Petoskey still has its share of necessary services, from post offices to pharmacies. For banking needs, contact **Chase** (www.chase.com) and **Fifth Third Bank** (www.53.com), both of which have several branches in Petoskey. For medical services, consult the **Northern Michigan Regional Hospital** (416 Connable Ave., 800/248-6777, www.northernhealth.org). If an emergency occurs, don't hesitate to call **911** from any phone.

GETTING THERE AND AROUND
As with other coastal resort towns in the northwestern part of Michigan's Lower Peninsula, Petoskey isn't terribly hard to reach. First of all, given its position beside Little Traverse Bay, it's obviously accessible by boat. In addition, visitors can reach Petoskey via bus; both **Greyhound** (231/439-0747 or 800/231-2222, www.greyhound.com) and **Indian Trails** (800/292-3831, www.indiantrails.com) regularly stop in town, specifically in front of the

restaurant located at 2286 Harbor Petoskey Road.

Another option is to fly into the region. Nearby airports include **Pellston Regional Airport** (PLN, 1395 US-31, Pellston, 231/539-8441 or 231/539-8442, www.pellstonairport.com), which is located northeast of Petoskey and offers commuter service from Detroit via Delta Air Lines, and **Cherry Capital Airport** (TVC, 727 Fly Don't Dr., Traverse City, 231/947-2250, www.tvcairport.com), which is situated in Traverse City and offers commuter service from Detroit and Minneapolis via Delta Air Lines and from Chicago via United Airlines and American Airlines. From either airport, you can rent a vehicle and take US-31 to Petoskey. From the Pellston airport, for instance, you'll take US-31 South to downtown Petoskey; without traffic, the 20-mile trip should take about 28 minutes. From the Traverse City airport, meanwhile, you'll take CR-620, 3 Mile Road, and US-31 North to reach Petoskey; without traffic, the 65-mile trip usually takes about 80 minutes.

Of course, most visitors come by car, which is an ideal way to explore the surrounding towns and lakes. From Sault Ste. Marie, for instance, you'll take I-75 South, cross the Mackinac Bridge (a toll bridge), and merge onto US-31 South to reach Petoskey, a 93-mile trip that normally takes about 1.75 hours. From downtown Detroit, meanwhile, you can follow I-375 North to I-75 North, take M-32 West, follow US-131 North, and continue to US-31 North toward downtown Petoskey; without traffic, the 268-mile trip will require about 4 hours. No matter how you reach Petoskey, though, you can easily get around town via car, bike, or foot.

LITTLE TRAVERSE BAY
North of the Leelanau Peninsula and just a half hour south of the Straits of Mackinac, Little Traverse Bay delves due east nine miles, forming a picture-perfect bay ringed by bluffs, fine sand, and well-protected harbors. Well-known Petoskey, with its historic downtown Gaslight District, sits at the foot of the bay, justifiably

drawing many of the area's visitors. But golfers, skiers, anglers, and wanderers will find plenty to enjoy in this appealing and compact region, too.

LAKE MICHIGAN SHORE

Bay Harbor

A couple of miles west of downtown Petoskey, Bay Harbor represents the nation's largest land reclamation project, a stunning example of what foresight and $100 million can accomplish. Stretching five miles along the shore of Little Traverse Bay and encompassing more than 1,100 acres, this beautiful chunk of real estate spent its last life as, of all things, a cement plant. When the plant closed in 1981, it left behind a scarred, barren landscape that sat untouched for a decade.

But from industrial squalor comes impressive luxury. With the combined resources of CMS Energy (the Jackson, Michigan, parent company of a large utility) and ski-industry giant Boyne, Bay Harbor has shaped up into one of the nation's most spectacular resort communities. The **Bay Harbor Yacht Club,** with little touches like a compass rose made of inlaid cherrywood, overlooks a deepwater port (the old quarry) with nearly 500 slips, including 120 for public transient use. An equestrian club entertains the horsy set. Multimillion-dollar homes dot the property, at a low density that maintains a breezy, resort feel. Public parks buffer Bay Harbor on both sides.

Acclaimed golf designer Arthur Hills has created **The Links, The Preserve,** and **The Quarry golf courses** (5800 Coastal Ridge Dr., 231/439-4085, www.bayharborgolf. com, $39-159 pp), 27 holes that ramble atop 160-foot bluffs, over natural sand dunes, and along the shoreline for more than two miles. Eight holes hug the water—more, Boyne developers like to tell you, than at Pebble Beach. Completed in 1998, it was almost immediately named the eighth-best public course in the nation by *Golf Magazine.*

Bay View

Adjacent to Petoskey on the east side of town, Bay View looks like a Hollywood set for a Victorian romance. This amazing community includes 430 Victorian homes, most built before the 1900s, a riot of gingerbread trim and cotton-candy colors. All are on the National Historic Register, and represent the largest single collection of historic homes in the country.

Bay View was founded by the Methodist Church in 1875, a summer-only religious retreat that took some inspiration from the Chautauqua movement in the East. Summers at Bay View were filled with lectures, recitals, craft classes, and religious programs. Over the years, speakers included such notable names as Booker T. Washington, Helen Keller, and William Jennings Bryan.

Originally a tent community, Bay View's canvas lodgings were slowly replaced by Victorian cottages, many with grand views of Little Traverse Bay. Bay View residents were not an extremely wealthy lot; the homes come in all shapes and sizes, lined up in tidy rows in a shady, park-like campus. Residents own their cottages but lease the land from the Methodist Church.

Today, Bay View remains a quiet enclave, still hosting a full roster of courses, concerts, and other events. While many residents are descendants of Bay View's founding families, the strict religious focus has been diluted. The biggest emphasis now, it seems, is on carefully preserving Bay View's slice of history. (Even minor renovations require approval by the Bay View Association.) Plan a stroll or a bike ride through this calm, gentle place for a true taste of another era.

Petoskey State Park

Just beyond Bay View, **Petoskey State Park** (2475 M-119, Petoskey, 231/347-2311, annual $11 Recreation Passport for Michigan residents or $8.40 day-use fee/$30.50 yearly Recreation Passport for nonresidents required) bends along the east end of Little Traverse Bay. Though quite small at 300 acres, the park nonetheless offers a nice dose of nature right smack between the summertime bustle of Petoskey and Harbor Springs. Its main attraction is its mile-long

PETOSKEY STONES

Michigan's official state stone isn't really a stone at all, but a chunk of fossilized coral more than 350 million years old. Coral reefs once thrived in the warm-water seas that covered northern Michigan from Grand Traverse Bay to Alpena on present-day Lake Huron. They are characterized by the distinct honeycomb pattern that covers them. Petoskey stones are common enough that they don't have much real value, but are prized nonetheless by rockhounds and anyone looking for a true local souvenir.

When dry, Petoskey stones often look like, well, ordinary stones, typically with a dusty gray-brown hue. Their unique pattern, however, becomes more apparent when they're wet and especially when polished. Since the stones are quite soft, locals suggest polishing them by hand with 220-grit wet sandpaper, then repeating the process with 400-grit and 600-grit sandpaper. Rock tumblers are not recommended.

Hunt for Petoskey stones along public beaches almost anywhere in the Traverse Bay region. Some of the more productive spots include Fisherman's Island State Park south of Charlevoix and Petoskey State Park beside Little Traverse Bay. You also can find Petoskey stones, polished up and often crafted into jewelry, at gift shops throughout the northwestern part of Michigan's Lower Peninsula.

---

beach, with soft sand and enough rocks to keep people on the hunt for Petoskey stones. (The coral pattern appears most clearly when wet, so dip a promising-looking stone in the water.) Try to look up occasionally; the beach has great views of Petoskey and Harbor Springs, and can serve up some terrific sunsets.

Climb the 0.7-mile **Old Baldy Trail** for an even better view from the top of a dune. The park's only other hiking trail, the **Portage Trail,** is an easy 2.8-mile loop that winds south to a little inland lake. It's groomed in winter for cross-country skiing.

Nearly 200 modern campsites are tucked behind some small dunes, mostly wooded sites with good privacy. Sites along the southern loop are closer to the bay, with a few prime (though more public) sites right on the water.

Harbor Springs

Just before Petoskey State Park, US-31 veers inland toward Mackinaw City and the straits. To stay along the water, turn west on M-119, which follows the curve of Little Traverse Bay and traces the Lower Peninsula's final stretch of Lake Michigan shoreline.

If you were to imagine the quintessential summer resort getaway, it might look a lot like genteel Harbor Springs on the north side of Little Traverse Bay: a deep, clear harbor tucked against a high, wooded bluff, ringed with grand estates and white church spires and, for good measure, gleaming yachts bobbing at anchor.

Harbor Springs, in fact, has the deepest natural harbor on all of the Great Lakes, which made it a natural stopping point for the large passenger steamers in the early 1900s. Several artesian wells added to its appeal, making it a popular destination for those seeking healthful air and water. Families like the Fords and the Gambles (of "Proctor and" fame) decided Harbor Springs looked pretty good and helped create exclusive resort communities like Harbor Point and Wequetonsing, where crisp white mansions line up across crisp emerald lawns.

Those "old money" communities still thrive, now inhabited largely by younger generations of Fords and Gambles. Harbor Point remains the more exclusive of the two, with homes topping $10 million hidden away behind gates. The only way in and out is by foot or carriage; even cars are banned from the point. You can walk, bike, or drive through Wequetonsing (WEE-kwee to the locals), where homes have wonderfully nostalgic names like Summer Set and Brookside, and long lines of Adirondack chairs line up on porches, just in case 10 or 12 friends drop by for gin and tonics.

It all makes for an interesting diversity, where ultra-wealthy Old Guard, younger trust-funders, vacationing families, and hired help all commingle easily in the delightfully tidy downtown. Of course, Harbor Springs has no strip malls, no sprawl, no ugly franchise signs.

Shopping is a popular sport in Harbor Springs, which hosts an appealing mix of galleries, tony boutiques, and distinctive hand-made crafts. Start your exploring at Main and State. Also check out the **Harbor Springs History Museum** (349 E. Main St., 231/526-9771, www.harborspringshistory.org, 11am-3pm Fri.-Sat., by appointment 9am-5pm Tues.-Thurs., 9am-11am and 3pm-5pm Fri., $5 adults, $3 seniors and children), which uses photographs, artifacts, and hands-on activities to explore the area's history, from the influence of the Odawa Indians to the emergence of the ski industry. Here, you'll also learn about famous former residents, such as Andrew J. Blackbird, an Odawa chief who lived here in the mid-1800s. The town's first postmaster, Blackbird wrote books about Indian language, legends, and adapting to white civilization.

The harborfront is a natural for strolling, with ample benches and a swimming beach at **Zorn Park** near the west end. (Hardy bathers only—the harbor's water is *cold*.) For a more natural beach, the **Thorne Swift Nature Preserve** (231/347-0991 or 231/526-6401, www.landtrust.org) offers a quiet 300-foot sand beach and dune observation deck with a wonderful bay view. Other trails wind through cedar lowlands, with trees canted and curved at crazy angles, and are marked with interpretive signs. A protected holding of the very active Little Traverse Conservancy, Thorne Swift has a naturalist on duty daily Memorial Day-Labor Day. Pick a breezy day to visit, since bugs can be zealous here in summer months. To reach the preserve from Harbor Springs, head northwest on M-119 for 3.8 miles and then follow Lower Shore Drive for a half-mile. The preserve sign will be on your left.

Tunnel of Trees

The stretch of M-119 from Harbor Springs to Cross Village is considered one of the prettiest drives in Michigan, and deserves the distinction. The narrow lane twists and turns as it follows Lake Michigan from high atop a bluff, with furtive views of the water and the Beaver Island archipelago. Yet it is the trees that take top billing, arching overhead to form a sun-dappled tunnel. The effect is spectacular on autumn afternoons, when the fiery oranges and bronzes glow in the angled sunlight like hot coals.

In spring, trilliums form a blanket of white on the forest floor. Spring also offers a few more deep blue glimpses of the lake, since the trees usually are not fully leafed out until late May. And any season is a good time to spot wildlife. One trip up the corkscrewy road tallied five deer, 15 wild turkeys, and countless grouse.

Try to bike or drive this road during the week, or at least early or late in the day, when traffic should be lighter. The combination of narrow blacktop, blind curves, no shoulders, and lots of wildlife means you'll need to keep a close eye on the road. The more cars there are, the less scenery you can enjoy.

Legs Inn

Even if you've traveled far and wide, it's doubtful you've ever encountered anything like the **Legs Inn** (6425 N. Lake Shore Dr., Cross Village, 231/526-2281, www.legsinn.com, 11am-9pm daily, $14-25). Part ethnic restaurant, part eclectic folk art display, this is a weird and fascinating place to explore. Outside is strange enough, a roadside building with a facade of fieldstone, accented with bizarre-looking totems and carved wooden legs spiking up from the roof (hence, the "legs" name).

But that's nothing compared with the interior, where the bar is a dark and mysterious den crammed with twisted driftwood, roots, and stumps-turned-cocktail tables. Seemingly every square inch has been carved into fanciful shapes, weird faces, and indescribable animals—and more and more seem to appear as your eyes adjust to the darkness. The theme carries through to the dining rooms, though not with such intensity. These areas are brighter and warmer, with picture windows overlooking gardens and distant views of Lake Michigan.

Legs Inn was created by Stanley Smolak, a Polish immigrant who moved to Cross Village from Chicago in the 1920s. He became enamored with the local land and its native people. He befriended the local Ottawa tribes, still thriving here in the 1920s, and was accepted enough into their culture that they gave him an Indian name, Chief White Cloud. Inspired by their art, he began carving. Soon, word of his restaurant and his relations with the Indians made Smolak a celebrity back in Poland.

With its eccentric decor, it's almost easy to overlook the food at the Legs Inn, but you shouldn't. It offers a wonderful array of Polish cooking, with rich soups, thick stews, and popular Polish specialties like pierogies. Even the drink menu offers Polish vodkas and Polish meads, made from honey and fruit juices. This is authentic stuff—many of the cook staff are immigrants themselves. They'll smile and nod and feed you like long-lost relatives.

Sturgeon Bay

M-119 ends at Cross Village, but continue northeast on Scenic Route 1 along Sturgeon Bay to reach **Bliss Township Park,** with low dunes and a pretty sand beach, great for swimming and sunsets. Far enough away from Petoskey and the Straits of Mackinac, it rarely draws a crowd.

Sturgeon Bay also offers the best big-water windsurfing in the area, with an easy shore break and generally warmer water than Little Traverse Bay. Bliss Township Park is a wonderful launch in southwest through north winds. A second launch is about a mile north of the township beach, just where the road makes a hard right. Watch for poison ivy. Advanced sailors looking for big waves should check out the boat launch in Cross Village—good in west through north winds.

Wilderness State Park

North of Cross Village near the top of the "mitten," Waugoshance Point stretches west out into Lake Michigan and dribbles off into a series of islands. This is the spectacular setting for **Wilderness State Park** (903 Wilderness Park Dr., Carp Lake, 231/436-5381, annual $11 Recreation Passport for Michigan residents or $8.40 day-use fee/$30.50 yearly Recreation Passport for nonresidents required), the second-largest state park in the Lower Peninsula. Aptly named, it occupies more than 7,500 acres of largely undeveloped land, including more than 26 miles of Lake Michigan shoreline. Considering that it sits just 15 minutes away from the Straits of Mackinac, it offers remarkable solitude.

As proof, this is one of the nesting sites of the endangered piping plover. (When the birds are nesting in late spring and early summer, part of the point is closed to visitors.) About 100 other bird species also nest or migrate through Wilderness State Park, making it a favorite of bird-watchers. Anglers also gather here, with notable bass fishing especially in the grassy beds along the southern shore of the point. The park has a boat launch near the campgrounds and day-use area.

The park offers a wide range of topography, with sandy beaches and rocky limestone ledges along the shore. Inland, 12 miles of trails (mostly old truck trails) wind through cedars, pines, and birches. A gravel road leads toward the end of the point, open to autos. To hike there, you can follow the northern shoreline for two miles, unless the endangered piping plovers are nesting. Depending on weather conditions and water depths, it's often possible to wade to Temperance Island—a fun mini-adventure.

Wilderness State Park has two large campgrounds with 250 sites, five rustic cabins, and 24-bunk lodges for rent ($12-69 daily). The Lakeshore Campground sits on Big Stone Bay in an open, grassy setting, with several sites right along the water. Just across the park road, the Pines Campground has more shaded, private sites in the, uh, pines.

MACKINAC ISLAND AND NORTHEAST MICHIGAN

Commonly called the Sunrise Side, the northeastern part of Michigan's Lower Peninsula is perhaps its most under-appreciated region—which is a shame given the untamed beauty that abounds here. Of course, year-round residents and seasonal vacationers value the tranquility of this less traveled place, so most are grateful that development has been slower here than in other parts of Michigan.

The area's remarkable woods—including sizable Hartwick Pines State Park—lure a wide array of recreationists, from hikers in summer to hunters in winter, while the region's many lakes, such as Higgins Lake south of Grayling, attract numerous anglers, boaters, and canoeists. Wildlife enthusiasts relish Northeast Michigan, too—it's common to spot scurrying foxes amid the underbrush, curious deer along country roads, bald eagles circling above the coves, and majestic elk stalking through the Pigeon River Country State Forest, home to the largest free-roaming elk herd east of the Mississippi River.

Although many locals live here all year long—even during the splendid, if bitter cold, winters—more come during the summer months, escaping humid places like Chicago and Florida. Dwelling in vacation cottages that line the roads and encircle the area's idyllic lakes, these seasonal residents spend their summers playing golf, shopping for antiques, fishing for walleye, and picking wild blueberries.

A superb way to experience the hinterlands of Northeast Michigan is, ironically, via the road. The 22-mile River Road Scenic Byway showcases the high cliffs, white pines, and wooded

© DREAMSTIME.COM

HIGHLIGHTS

LOOK FOR ◖ TO FIND RECOMMENDED SIGHTS, ACTIVITIES, DINING, AND LODGING.

◖ **Colonial Michilimackinac State Historic Park:** Just south of the Mackinac Bridge lies this reconstruction of the original Fort Michilimackinac, a French fur-trading village and military outpost established in 1715. Costumed soldiers, traders, and colonial ladies demonstrate skills of the late 18th century (page 63).

◖ **Grand Hotel:** Opened in 1887, this gorgeous hotel is a timeless piece of American history, boasting the world's longest porch and a guest list that's included at least five U.S. presidents (page 71).

◖ **Diving in Thunder Bay:** Scuba divers will discover a wealth of artifacts in the 448-square-mile Thunder Bay National Marine Sanctuary and Underwater Preserve. "Shipwreck Alley" is the unfortunate resting place of more than 80 historic vessels (page 83).

◖ **Canoeing on the Au Sable River:** Home to North America's longest nonstop canoe marathon, the Au Sable is one of the most picturesque rivers in Michigan (page 88).

◖ **Houghton and Higgins Lakes:** These sizable inland lakes, two of the state's largest, offer seven swimming beaches, nearly a dozen access sites for boaters and anglers in summer, and the possibility of ice fishing for walleye, pike, bass, and bluegill in winter (page 93).

◖ **Hartwick Pines State Park:** One of the largest state parks also preserves the state's largest remaining stand of virgin white pines. View forestry exhibits, experience a former logging camp, explore trails, and observe a variety of wildlife (page 98).

◖ **Golfing in Gaylord:** Golfers will find a wide assortment of options in the northern half of the Lower Peninsula, especially in the area around Gaylord, which offers a high concentration of championship golf courses, with challenging holes, scenic views, and fine lodgings (page 101).

lakes of the Au Sable River Valley. Meanwhile, the Sunrise Side Coastal Highway (US-23) stretches for 200 miles along the Lake Huron shoreline, from Standish to the Mackinac Bridge. Along the way, motorists can experience quaint coastal towns, inviting beaches, and lovely lighthouses. These stunning drives are especially wonderful in the fall, when the trees are ablaze with spectacular colors.

Situated just north of the mainland lies Mackinac Island, a nostalgic destination claimed by both the Upper and Lower Peninsulas. Although most of the island is preserved as a state park, about 20 percent of it

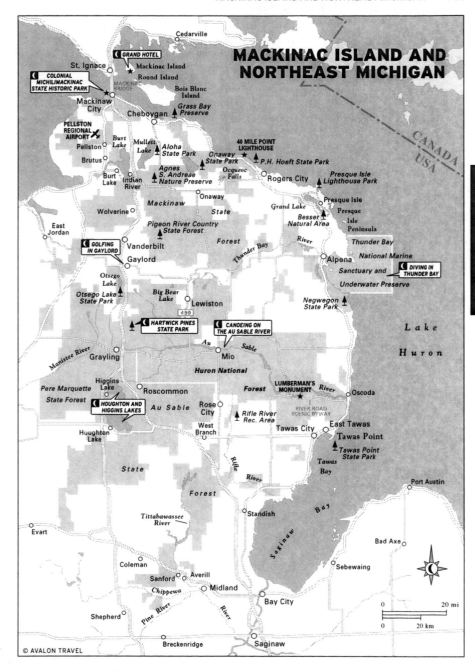

MACKINAC ISLAND AND NORTHEAST MICHIGAN

Cedarville

(GRAND HOTEL

St. Ignace · Mackinac Island

(COLONIAL MICHILIMACKINAC STATE HISTORIC PARK

Round Island

MACKINAC BRIDGE

Bois Blanc Island

Mackinaw City

Cheboygan · Grass Bay Preserve

PELLSTON REGIONAL AIRPORT

Burt Lake · Mullett Lake

Pellston

Aloha State Park

Onaway State Park

40 MILE POINT LIGHTHOUSE

Brutus

P.H. Hoeft State Park

Burt Lake · Indian River

Agnes S. Andreae Nature Preserve

Ocqueoc Falls

Rogers City

Presque Isle Lighthouse Park

Onaway

Wolverine

Mackinaw

State

Grand Lake

Presque Isle

Besser Natural Area

Presque Isle Peninsula

CANADA

USA

East Jordan

Pigeon River Country State Forest

Forest

River

Thunder Bay

(GOLFING IN GAYLORD

Vanderbilt

Thunder Bay

Alpena

Thunder Bay National Marine Sanctuary and Underwater Preserve

(DIVING IN THUNDER BAY

Gaylord

Otsego Lake

Otsego Lake State Park

Big Bear Lake

Lewiston

489

Negwegon State Park

Lake Huron

(HARTWICK PINES STATE PARK

(CANOEING ON THE AU SABLE RIVER

Au

Sable

Manistee River

Grayling

Mio

Huron National

Higgins Lake

Pere Marquette State Forest

Roscommon

Forest

LUMBERMAN'S MONUMENT

River

Oscoda

(HOUGHTON AND HIGGINS LAKES

Au Sable

Rose City

Rifle River Rec. Area

RIVER ROAD SCENIC BYWAY

Houghton Lake

West Branch

Tawas City

East Tawas

Tawas Point

Tawas Point State Park

State

Rifle

River

Tawas Bay

Port Austin

Forest

Tittabawassee River

Standish

Bay

Saginaw

Evart

Bad Axe

Coleman

Sebewaing

Sanford · Averill

Chippewa

Midland

Bay City

0   20 mi

Shepherd

Pine River

River

0   20 km

Breckenridge

Saginaw

has become a year-round tourist mecca, offering boat docks, historic sites, enchanting hotels, and intriguing attractions like the Original Butterfly House & Insect World. Since automobiles are banned here, bikes, horses, and carriages are the preferred modes of transportation—just another facet of the island's yesteryear vibe. Mackinac Island might be, at times, teeming with "fudgies" (a local term for tourists), but its charms are unmistakable, and it's definitely worth a look after exploring the wilds of Northeast Michigan.

PLANNING YOUR TIME

For those who prefer small towns, the solitude of the great outdoors, and winter activities like snowmobiling, Northeast Michigan is an ideal precursor to visiting the even wilder and more isolated Upper Peninsula. In the summer, it's also a good spot to avoid the crowded beaches and resort towns along Lake Michigan. Of course, that doesn't mean you won't encounter plenty of folks on the area's championship golf courses, near inland lakes during summer weekends, and on Mackinac Island throughout the year. You will, however, likely avoid crowds during the off-season, November-March.

To hit the highlights of Northeast Michigan, you'll need a minimum of three days, including a day trip to Mackinac Island. A whole week will give you a better chance to tour the historic coastline and explore the interior's impressive forests and lakes.

Two main roads cut through the Huron shore region. US-23 hugs the coastline from Standish to the Straits of Mackinac, offering vistas and villages along the way. I-75 is the quicker, though less scenic, route, heading north from Bay City, through Grayling and Gaylord, to the Mackinac Bridge.

For those not driving to Northeast Michigan (or arriving via private boat), consider taking a Greyhound bus to towns like Cheboygan, Rogers City, Alpena, Tawas City, Grayling, and Gaylord. It's also possible to fly into the Pellston Regional Airport and Alpena County Regional Airport, both of which are served by Delta Air Lines. If you plan on exploring several areas in this spread-out region, it's advisable to rent a vehicle as soon as you arrive.

Tourism folks market the Huron shore region as the state's "Sunrise Side." For more information about Northeast Michigan, consult **Travel Michigan** (Michigan Economic Development Corporation, 300 N. Washington Sq., Lansing, 888/784-7328, www.michigan.org) or the **Northern Michigan Tourist Association** (www.travelnorth.org).

HISTORY

In appearance, Northeast Michigan has come nearly full circle in 200 years. Its first inhabitants were Native Americans, who left the land much as they found it, until the Europeans arrived in the 17th century. By the mid-1800s, logging companies that had exhausted the nation's eastern forests had moved on to Michigan's fertile ground, making it the largest lumber-producing state in the country between 1850 and 1910, with an estimated 700 logging camps and more than 2,000 mills.

Before the rush of settlers to Michigan in the 1830s, more than 13 million of the state's 37 million acres were covered with white pine. These majestic trees thrived in sandy soil, grew up to 200 feet tall, and could live an incredible 500 years. By 1900, however, all that was left of these once awe-inspiring forests were stumps. Logging had devastated the terrain, leaving behind a wasteland.

In 1909, the federal government established the Huron National Forest, the first of many such preserves that sought to repair years of damage. More than a century later, much of this region is once again forested, and it's possible to hike for miles through towering, whispering pines.

Mackinac Island, of course, has its own unique history. The Ojibwa and Ottawa peoples called it Michilimackinac, which some scholars claim means "The Great Turtle," an apt description for this hump of limestone. The Indians summered here, hunting, fishing, and trading some of their catch for grains and produce from other tribes.

French missionaries were the first Europeans to settle in the area, erecting a mission in nearby St. Ignace in 1671. The French were also the first whites to exploit the rich fur harvest, establishing a trading post in St. Ignace in the late 1600s. In 1715, they erected Fort Michilimackinac in Mackinaw City. The British, meanwhile, were also eager to expand their territory. They regularly skirmished with the French, and Fort Michilimackinac traded hands more than once—that is, until the 1763 Treaty of Paris gave all French land east of the Mississippi to Great Britain.

Upstart colonists became the new enemy. In 1780, the British commander abandoned Fort Michilimackinac in favor of Mackinac Island, where the high limestone bluffs offered better protection from attack. Though American troops never came, they won the fort anyway, gaining title to the northern territory after the American Revolution. Still, the British refused to turn over the fort until 1796.

During the War of 1812, British troops landed at the northern end of the island in early morning darkness, dragged a couple of cannons up the bluff and aimed them at Fort Mackinac below. The surprised Americans surrendered without firing a single shot. The British once again controlled Fort Mackinac until 1814,

when the Treaty of Ghent passed the land back to the United States once and for all.

In 1817, John Jacob Astor set up the American Fur Company here, bartering with the Indians for beaver pelts and storing them in warehouses on the island. Until overhunting decimated the fur industry and commercial fishing became the area's mainstay, Astor ranked as the richest man in the United States.

By the second half of the 19th century, Mackinac Island had evolved from a battleground to a gracious getaway. Wealthy Midwesterners, who had heard about the island's lovely waters and clean air, began arriving by lake steamer to summer here. Hotels sprang up, soon followed by private homes along the bluffs—30-room Victorian "cottages," complete with carriage houses, stables, and servants' quarters.

To minimize its potentially destructive impact, the automobile was banned from Mackinac Island as quickly as it arrived. Today, roughly 600 horses are stabled on the island in summer, used for hauling freight, pulling carriages, and private recreation. The horses, carts, carriages, bicycle fleets, and well-preserved Victorians all blend to give Mackinac the magical, frozen-in-time feel that has turned it into one of the most popular vacation spots in the Midwest.

NORTHEAST MICHIGAN

Mackinaw City

Although some may consider it a tourist trap, Mackinaw City offers more than just strip malls and souvenir shops. Despite overdevelopment, the town has several things to recommend it—namely, a maritime museum, a lighthouse, two excellent historic parks, several fudge shops, numerous hotel rooms, terrific views of the Great Lakes, and, of course, ferry service to Mackinac Island.

SIGHTS
◖ Colonial Michilimackinac State Historic Park

Archaeologists have been uncovering treasures since 1959 on the site of this 18th-century fur-trading post, believed to be the nation's longest-running archaeological dig. It was long a well-traveled Indian hunting and trading ground, and the French built a post here in 1715. The French exploited the Indians, bribing them with gifts and alcohol,

© MACKINAC STATE HISTORIC PARKS

a period gardener at Colonial Michilimackinac State Historic Park

and encouraging them to work in the fur trade. Though the unfortunate relationship led many Indians to abandon their traditional way of life, the two groups rarely fought. Instead, the French feuded with the British, who sought to expand their landholdings in the region. For the next 65 years, the fort along the straits alternately fell under French and British control.

The fort's most violent episode occurred while it was under British rule. In 1763, Pontiac, the Ottawa war chief, ordered an attack on British posts all over Michigan, an attempt to drive the growing British population out of their native land. While Pontiac laid siege to Detroit, local Ojibwa stormed the fort, killing all but 13 soldiers. In the end, though, it was the feisty colonists who sent the British fleeing from Fort Michilimackinac. They dismantled what they could and burned the rest to the ground in 1780, opting for a new, more-defensible post on nearby Mackinac Island.

Today, **Colonial Michilimackinac State Historic Park** (102 W. Straits Ave., 231/436-4100, www.mackinacparks.com, 9am-6pm daily June-Aug., 9am-4pm daily May and Sept.-mid-Oct., $10 adults, $6.25 children 5-17), located just west of the Mackinac Bridge, portrays the lives of both the Indians and European settlers, with costumed interpreters reenacting daily life at an Indian encampment and a stockaded fort. Displays include many of the artifacts unearthed by archaeologists. Interpreters demonstrate various crafts and skills, from cooking and weaving to cleaning weapons. Interpreters are quite knowledgeable and able to answer most visitors' questions. Don't miss the underground archaeological tunnel exhibit, "Treasures from the Sand."

Historic Mill Creek Discovery Park

Today, this exceptionally pretty glen and rushing stream creates a pleasant oasis for visitors, but it once was an innovative industrial site. When the British made plans to move from Fort Michilimackinac to Mackinac Island, Scotsman Robert Campbell recognized their imminent need for lumber. He purchased 640 acres of the land around the only waterway in the area with enough flow to power a sawmill. He built the mill in 1790 and later added a blacksmith shop and gristmill.

The site was no longer profitable when the fort ceased operation, so it was abandoned in the mid-1800s. Since the 1970s, archaeologists and historians have worked together to re-create the water-powered sawmill on its original site. Today, visitors to the 625-acre **Historic Mill Creek Discovery Park** (9001 US-23, 231/436-4100, www.mackinacparks.com, 9am-5pm daily June-Aug., 9am-4pm daily May and Sept.-mid-Oct., $7.50 adults, $4.50 children 5-17) can see the splashing waterwheel in action and visit the Orientation Center, which has an audiovisual presentation and displays on other artifacts uncovered during the dig. Make sure to walk the park's 1.5 miles of trails, which wind along the creek and mill pond, rising up to scenic overlooks with views of the straits and Mackinac Island.

Old Mackinac Point Lighthouse

Located on a point just east of the Mackinac Bridge, this 1892 cream-brick light guided ships through the busy Straits of Mackinac for nearly 70 years. When the Mackinac Bridge was completed in 1957, it became obsolete, since vessels could range on the bridge's high lights instead of the diminutive 40-foot tower. Today, the charming **Old Mackinac Point Lighthouse** (9am-5pm daily June-Aug., 9am-4pm daily May and Sept.-mid-Oct., $6 adults, $3.50 children 5-17), topped with a cherry-red roof, houses a maritime museum, part of Colonial Michilimackinac State Historic Park. A schooner and other ships are docked and on display. The lighthouse grounds serve as their own delightful little park, with impressive views of the Mackinac Bridge as well as picnic tables scattered around a tidy lawn.

From here, you can reach several island and offshore reef lights via boat—though you should take care in these potentially dangerous waters. Two of the most interesting are the 1874 **Spectacle Reef Light,** an impressive example of a monolithic stone lighthouse, and the 1895 **Round Island Light** in the Straits of Mackinac.

the Old Mackinac Point Lighthouse

NORTHEAST MICHIGAN

Mackinac Bridgemen Museum

It's not slick or fancy, but the small **Bridgemen Museum** (231 E. Central, 231/436-8751, 8am-midnight daily May-Oct., free) above Mama Mia's Pizza is loaded with tidbits and artifacts on the construction of the $100 million Mackinac Bridge. A very well-done video documents the bridge's design and construction. For more information about the bridge itself, consult the **Mackinac Bridge Authority** (www.mackinacbridge.org).

Lighthouse Tours

Although a self-guided tour of Michigan's lighthouses can be a delightful way to pass a few days in the Great Lakes State, the experience can be even more enlightening with a well-informed guide. Besides shuttling tourists to and from Mackinac Island, **Shepler's Mackinac Island Ferry** (800/828-6157, www.sheplersferry.com) also offers lighthouse cruises ($52.50 adults, $27.50 children 5-12). Departing from Mackinaw City, these trips guide passengers amid lighthouses and shipwrecks that would be difficult for most people to reach otherwise. Along the way, passengers are treated to historical tales that provide an informative context for the lighthouses that still stand today. The eastbound cruise features offshore lights like Round Island Light and the privately owned Bois Blanc Island Light, while the westbound cruise highlights structures such as the red-and-white-striped White Shoal Light and the 1873 St. Helena Island Lighthouse.

SHOPPING

Although Mackinaw City isn't as high on shoppers' lists as, for instance, the resort towns along Lake Michigan, it does have its share of decent shops. Of course, no area is quite as pleasant as **Mackinaw Crossings** (248 S. Huron Ave., 231/436-5030, www.mackinawcrossings.com, shop hours vary), a tidy open-air collection of restaurants and stores. Here, you can find everything from **To Bead or Not to Bead,** which offers handmade jewelry and beads for creating your own accessories, to the **Great Lakes**

Mackinaw City shops

© DANIEL MARTONE

Bear Factory, where children (and adults) can customize their very own stuffed teddy bears.

ACCOMMODATIONS AND FOOD

With the Straits of Mackinac a major tourism draw, Mackinaw City alone has more than 3,000 rooms. For a variety of amenities, check out the **Comfort Inn Lakeside** (611 S. Huron Ave., 231/436-5057, www.comfortinn.com, $158-220 d) or the **Ramada Inn Waterfront** (723 S. Huron Ave., 231/436-5055, www.ramadainn.com, $48-278 d).

In between sightseeing and shopping, grab a bite to eat at one of the numerous area restaurants. Step back a couple of centuries at the **Dixie Saloon** (401 E. Central Ave., 231/436-5449, www.dixiesaloon.com, 11am-9pm Sun.-Thurs., 11am-11pm Fri.-Sat., $6-24), a historic landmark. Try the potato-encrusted walleye or the fried perch, both of which are locally caught. For something a little more elegant, stop by **The Lighthouse Restaurant** (618 S. Huron Ave., 231/436-5191, 11am-9pm daily,

$10-49), with its prime rib, lobster, and excellent wine list.

INFORMATION AND SERVICES

For more information about Mackinaw City, contact the **Mackinaw Area Visitors Bureau** (231/436-5664, www.mackinawcity.com). While you won't find a ton of services here, there is indeed a small grocery, a post office, and a 24-hour ATM at **Citizens National Bank** (580 S. Nicolet St., 231/436-5271, www.cn-bismybank.com). In case of a police-related or medical emergency, dial **911** from any cell or public phone.

GETTING THERE AND AROUND

While Mackinaw City may not have any airports, train stations, or bus centers of its own, it's still not terribly difficult to reach the Lower Peninsula's northernmost town. **Pellston Regional Airport** (PLN, 1395 US-31, Pellston, 231/539-8441 or 231/539-8442, www.pellstonairport.com), for instance, offers commuter service from Detroit via Delta Air Lines. From there, you can rent a vehicle from Avis or Hertz, take US-31 North, merge onto I-75 North, and head north to downtown Mackinaw City; without traffic, the 16-mile trip should take about 20 minutes. With advance reservations, you can also hop aboard a van or shuttle bus via **Mackinaw Shuttle** (231/539-7005 or 888/349-8294, www.mackinawshuttle.com), which regularly transports passengers from the Pellston airport to Mackinaw City as well as other towns in northern Michigan, from Traverse

City and Petoskey in the Lower Peninsula to St. Ignace and Sault Ste. Marie in the Upper Peninsula.

Of course, many visitors come to Michigan by car, and luckily, it's possible to reach Mackinaw City from a variety of directions, usually via US-31, I-75, or US-23. From Sault Ste. Marie, for instance, you can simply take I-75 South to St. Ignace, cross the Mackinac Bridge (for which you'll have to pay a toll), and take exit 338 toward US-23; the 59-mile trip typically takes about an hour. From Traverse City, meanwhile, you can take US-31 North, merge onto I-75 North, and take exit 338 toward South Nicolet Street; without traffic, the 103-mile trip should take roughly two hours. Even downtown Detroit is closer to Mackinaw City than one might think; the 289-mile journey is predominantly a direct route via I-75 North, and without traffic, it usually takes about four hours to make the trip "up north."

If, on the other hand, you're coming from Chicago, you'll just take I-90 East and I-94 East through Illinois and Indiana, cross the Michigan state line, continue onto I-196 North/US-31 North and I-196 East, merge onto US-131 North, follow CR-42 and M-32 East, and take I-75 North to exit 338; without traffic, the 406-mile trip will require at least six hours. Just be advised that, en route from the Windy City, parts of I-90 East and I-94 East serve as the Indiana Toll Road. Still, no matter how you reach Mackinaw City, you may be happy to know that it's a fairly small town, so just park your vehicle and take a pleasant stroll amid the downtown shops and eateries.

Mackinac Island

Linking Lakes Huron and Michigan, the Straits of Mackinac (MAK-i-naw) have been a crossroads of the Great Lakes for hundreds of years, a key waterway for hunting, fishing, trading, and transportation. The four-mile-wide straits also sever Michigan in two, both emotionally and geographically. Until the 1950s, the only way across was by ferry, effectively blocking the development of the Upper Peninsula and creating half-day backups at the ferry dock during prime hunting and fishing seasons.

Today, the magnificent five-mile-long Mackinac Bridge stitches the state together, allowing a free flow between the Upper and Lower Peninsulas. But the straits, now a key vacation area for much of the Midwest, continue to lure people, and many come specifically for Mackinac Island.

No place name in Michigan conjures up as much history, attention, and affection as the tiny parcel known as Mackinac Island. Over the centuries, the 2,200-acre island has been a sacred ground for the Native Americans who summered here, an important base for French fur trappers, a fort for British soldiers, and a gilded summer retreat for the wealthiest of Victorian-era industrialists.

It is the Victorian era that Mackinac chose to preserve, from the exquisite 1887 Grand Hotel, with its 660-foot-long porch stretching across the hillside, to the clopping of the horse-drawn carriages down the vehicle-free streets. Yes, it can seem touristy at first blush. Yes, it can be crowded. But Mackinac Island can also be irrepressibly charming, all buffed up and neatly packaged, the state's heirloom jewel.

Some of the criticism lobbed at Mackinac is based on misconception, anyway. For starters, Mackinac is more than the tangle of fudge and souvenir shops that greet you at the ferry dock. A full 80 percent of the island is a state park, comprising a restored 18th-century fort, undeveloped woodlands, crisscrossing trails,

rare wildflowers, and sculpted limestone outcroppings.

Secondly, Mackinac Island has far more lodging choices than the famous Grand Hotel. Many are moderately priced. Plan to spend at least one night, so you have a little time to wander around and get past the cliché. Mackinac doesn't lend itself well to a cursory glance. Like those wealthy resorters knew, it's a wonderful place to retreat from the pulls of the real world.

SIGHTS

Downtown

Everyone wants to wander among the four blocks of shops and restaurants on Main Street. The ferry docks themselves are particularly interesting. At the Arnold Transit dock, you can sneak a peek at the day-to-day grunt work of Mackinac, like workers unloading carton after carton of vegetables from the ferry and reloading them by hand onto drays (wagons) for horse-drawn delivery to area restaurants. Even the UPS man does his route via bike, pulling a cart loaded with packages.

Once you've done the Main Street stroll and nibbled your requisite hunk of fudge (there's a reason tourists are known as "fudgies"), make the most of your visit by getting off the main drag. You can get a good taste of what the island has to offer on a carriage tour with **Mackinac Island Carriage Tours** (906/847-3307, www.mict.com, 9am-4pm daily May-Oct., $25 adults, $10 children 5-12), located across from the Arnold Transit ferry dock. The pleasant narrated tour takes about two hours, rambling along at a relaxing pace past the Grand Hotel, Arch Rock, Skull Cave, Fort Mackinac, and most of the island's other key sights. This locally owned business is the world's largest horse and buggy livery, with more than 300 horses, mostly crosses of beefy Percherons, Belgians, and Clydesdales.

One block inland from Main, some of Mackinac's original residences line up on

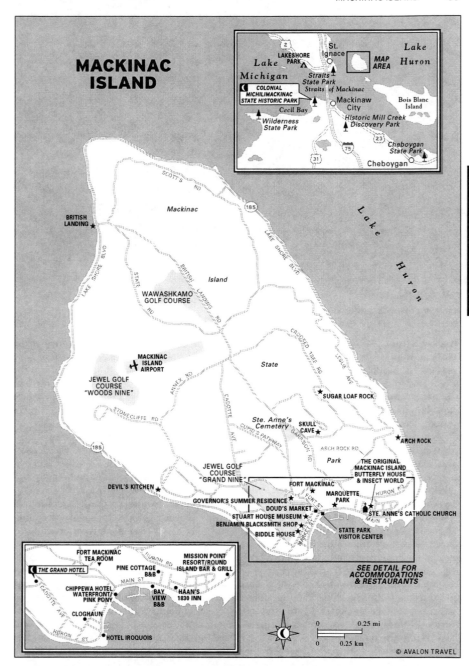

MACKINAC ISLAND

St. Ignace
Lake Michigan
LAKESHORE PARK
2
MAP AREA
Lake Huron
Straits State Park
COLONIAL MICHILIMACKINAC STATE HISTORIC PARK
Straits of Mackinac
Mackinaw City
Bois Blanc Island
Cecil Bay
Historic Mill Creek Discovery Park
Wilderness State Park
Cheboygan State Park
75
23
31
Cheboygan

SCOTT'S RD
Mackinac
185
BRITISH LANDING
Lake Huron
LAKE SHORE BLVD
Island
BRITISH LANDING RD
STATE
WAWASHKAMO GOLF COURSE
CROOKED TREE RD
MACKINAC ISLAND AIRPORT
State
ANNEX RD
LESLIE AVE
JEWEL GOLF COURSE "WOODS NINE"
CADOTTE AVE
STONECLIFFE RD
SUGAR LOAF ROCK
185
Ste. Anne's Cemetery
CUPID'S PATHWAY
SKULL CAVE
GARRISON RD
ARCH ROCK RD
ARCH ROCK
JEWEL GOLF COURSE "GRAND NINE"
Park
THE ORIGINAL MACKINAC ISLAND BUTTERFLY HOUSE & INSECT WORLD
DEVIL'S KITCHEN
FORT MACKINAC
MARQUETTE PARK
HURON RD
GOVERNOR'S SUMMER RESIDENCE
DOUD'S MARKET
FORT ST
STE. ANNE'S CATHOLIC CHURCH
STUART HOUSE MUSEUM
MAIN ST
BENJAMIN BLACKSMITH SHOP
BIDDLE HOUSE
STATE PARK VISITOR CENTER

SEE DETAIL FOR ACCOMMODATIONS & RESTAURANTS

FORT MACKINAC TEA ROOM
MISSION POINT RESORT/ROUND ISLAND BAR & GRILL
HURON RD
THE GRAND HOTEL
PINE COTTAGE B&B
CADOTTE AVE
MAIN ST
CHIPPEWA HOTEL WATERFRONT/ PINK PONY
BAY VIEW B&B
HAAN'S 1830 INN
CLOGHAUN
HURON
HOTEL IROQUOIS

0   0.25 mi
0   0.25 km

© AVALON TRAVEL

NORTHEAST MICHIGAN

© MACKINAC ISLAND TOURISM BUREAU

a horse-drawn carriage ride on Mackinac Island

Market Street. Much quieter than frenetic Main, Market has several interesting stops for visitors. The headquarters of the American Fur Company, John Jacob Astor's empire, is now the **Stuart House Museum** (34 Market St., 9am-4pm daily May-late Oct., donation suggested). The 1817 building retains much of its original decor, including fur company ledgers, fur weighing scales, and other artifacts. The museum is operated by the City of Mackinac Island.

A block west, knowledgeable interpreters demonstrate spinning at **Biddle House** and blacksmithing at the **Benjamin Blacksmith Shop** (both 11am-4pm daily mid-May-late Oct.). These and other historic buildings are part of the state park, and are included with the admission ticket to Fort Mackinac. For current information, stop by the park visitors center across from Marquette Park on Huron Street, or contact **Mackinac State Historic Parks** (213/436-4100, www.mackinacparks. com, 11am-4pm daily).

From Marquette Park, follow Fort Street up the hill to the **Governor's Residence** at the corner of Fort and East Bluff Road. The state purchased the "cottage" in the 1940s. It is the official summer residence of the governor, though the amount of time actually spent here varies from governor to governor. The house is open for tours on Wednesday mornings.

Some of the island's more impressive "cottages" line up along **East Bluff.** Wander east from the governor's mansion to see some of these Victorian marvels. Happily, most survived the Depression era—when they could be purchased for pennies on the dollar, of course. Today, they're well cared for and worth $1 million plus. (And remember, most are summer homes only!)

Work your way down one of the sets of public steps to the lakefront. Main Street has become Huron Street here. Continue your walk east, passing smaller but no less appealing cottages and homes. Many are skirted with geraniums and lilacs, the island's signature flowers. Behind Ste. Anne's Catholic Church, seek out the **Original Mackinac Island Butterfly House**

& Insect World (906/847-3972, www.original-butterflyhouse.com, 10am-7pm daily Memorial Day-Labor Day, $9 adults, $4.50 children 5-12), tucked away on McGulpin Street.

Owner Doug Beardsley used to use his greenhouses to grow thousands of geraniums for the Grand Hotel and others. He relied on biodynamic growing methods, releasing beneficial insects to care for his plants rather than chemical sprays. When economics made his small greenhouse less viable, he stuck with his insects. After hearing about a butterfly house in Europe, Beardsley added some different host plants and began ordering pupa from around the world. Now hundreds of butterflies fly freely in his greenhouse/atrium, some nearly six inches long. You can observe them up close on walls and plants, or sit still long enough and they'll land on you.

The engaging Beardsley hopes his attraction will help convince gardeners to wean themselves off herbicides and pesticides. He sells helpful insects to control garden pests like aphids and will give you ideas for attracting butterflies to your own garden. (Host plants like milkweed and cabbage, where butterflies like to lay their eggs, will work best. "Think of it as planting a caterpillar garden, not a butterfly garden," he says.)

❰ Grand Hotel

The **Grand Hotel** (286 Grand Ave., 906/847-3331 or 800/334-7263, www.grandhotel.com) has become practically synonymous with Mackinac Island, a gracious edifice built on a truly grand scale. It is the largest summer resort in the world, operating early May-late October. Its famous 660-foot-long covered front porch gets decked out each spring with 2,000 geraniums planted in seven *tons* of potting soil. Its 11 restaurants and bars serve as many as 4,000 meals a day. Its impeccable grounds offer guests every amenity, from saddle horses to designer golf to swimming in the outdoor pool made famous by the 1940s swimming actress, Esther Williams, who filmed *This Time for Keeps* here.

But opulence is what the railroads and

NORTHEAST MICHIGAN

© MACKINAC ISLAND TOURISM BUREAU

a busy day on Mackinac Island

NORTHEAST MICHIGAN

© MACKINAC STATE HISTORIC PARKS

costumed guides atop Fort Mackinac

steamships were after when they formed a consortium and built the Grand Hotel in 1887, dragging construction materials across the frozen waters by horse and mule. The wealthiest of all Mackinac Island visitors stayed here, of course, high on the hill.

Yet unlike other turn-of-the-20th-century resorts that burned to the ground or grew dog-eared and faded, the Grand Hotel has managed to maintain its grace and dignity over the years. It still hosts all manner of celebrities and politicians—five U.S. presidents to date—and still offers a sip of the Gilded Age, with high tea in the parlor each afternoon and demitasse served after dinner each evening. Room rates still include a five-course dinner in the soaring main dining room, and jackets/ties and skirts/dresses are still the required attire.

The Grand Hotel's time-capsule setting prompted director Jeannot Szwarc to choose it as the location for the 1980 film *Somewhere in Time,* starring Christopher Reeve, Jane Seymour, and Christopher Plummer. Curiously, the movie has developed a huge

following; its fan club reunites at the hotel each year in late October.

While room rates can get outright astronomical, they can be a worthwhile splurge if you enjoy this kind of thing. What the heck—take high tea, loll in the beautifully landscaped pool, or dance to the swing orchestra in the Terrace Room. Nonguests can sneak a peek at the hotel's public areas and grounds for a not-unreasonable $10. (It's needed to thin the sightseers more than anything.) Highly recommended are a stroll through the grounds, filled with Victorian gardens—24,000 tulips in spring!—and a visit to the snazzy Cupola Bar, with views halfway to Wisconsin.

Fort Mackinac

Located at the crest of the bluff, whitewashed **Fort Mackinac** (231/436-4100, 9am-5pm daily mid-May-mid-Oct., $10 adults, $6.25 children 6-17) is worth a visit for the views alone, presiding over—as forts do—the downtown, the marina, and Lake Huron. But there's also plenty to see at this military outpost, which the British and Americans haggled over for nearly 40 years.

Along with peering over the parapets, you can wander in and out of 14 buildings within the fort. The barracks, officers' quarters, post hospital, and others are filled with interpretive displays and decorated in period decor. Costumed guides lead all sorts of reenactments, including musket firings and cannon salutes. A short audiovisual presentation, "The Heritage of Mackinac," does a good job of presenting basic history.

Mackinac Island State Park

Often overshadowed by other visitor attractions, Mackinac Island's natural history has attracted scientific observation for over 200 years. In the early 19th century, botanists discovered several species completely new to science, including the dwarf lake iris, still found predominantly in the Straits of Mackinac region.

Early scientists also marveled at the island's distinctive geology, mostly brecciated limestone that has been sculpted by eons of wind and waves. The result is some dramatic rock formations, like the giant inland slab of limestone called Sugar Loaf Rock, the lakeside caves of Devil's Kitchen, and impressive Arch Rock, which rises nearly 150 feet above the eastern shore and spans some 50 feet.

In recognition of the park's distinctive natural curiosities and growing tourism, the U.S. government created Mackinac National Park in 1875—following Yellowstone as the nation's second national park. Twenty years later, it was returned to Michigan and became **Mackinac Island State Park** (906/847-3328, www.mackinacparks.com, park 24 hours daily, visitor's center 9am-4pm daily early May-early June and mid-Aug.-early Oct., 9am-6pm daily early June-mid-Aug., free), Michigan's first state park. For more information about the state park, head to the Mackinac Island Visitor's Center, on the south side of Main Street, across from Marquette Park.

SHOPPING

Although shopping isn't a huge activity here, the island does present a few unique browsing options. The **Island Scrimshander** (906/847-3792, www.scrimshanders.com, 9am-4pm daily May-Oct.), for instance, offers amazing engraved trinkets. You should also check out **La Galerie** (906/847-6311, 9am-4pm daily May-Oct.), with its line of Pandora jewelry and Christopher Radko ornaments.

RECREATION

Walk, run, bike, or ride a horse, but make sure you get out of downtown to really see Mackinac Island. You'll be surprised how quickly you can leave any crowds behind as you set out on the paved eight-mile path that circles the island. The trail never wanders far from the pleasant shoreline and passes many of the island's natural features, which are well marked. Traveling clockwise, the first you'll reach is Devil's Kitchen; heading in the opposite direction, you'll arrive first at Arch Rock, the most dramatic of all Mackinac limestone oddities.

About halfway around, on the island's northwestern side lies **British Landing,** where British soldiers sneaked onto the island in 1812. They hiked across Mackinac's interior, totally surprising the American garrison stationed at the fort (and apparently looking the other way), and recaptured the island. Today, the landing is a good spot for a picnic or short break (water and restrooms available). There's a small **nature center** here, staffed in summer months by a helpful naturalist. Hike the short nature trail, which has several interpretive signs as it weaves up a bluff.

British Landing is also a good spot from which to head inland and explore the island's interior. British Landing Road bisects the island and links up with Garrison Road near Skull Cave, leading to the fort. It's a hilly, three-mile trip from shore to shore. British Landing Road is considered a major road by Mackinac standards, meaning you'll share it with carriages. On bike or foot, you'll have endless other options—at last count, Mackinac had some 140 miles of trails and footpaths.

Pick up a free *Mackinac Island Map,* available all over town, and venture off. The map marks the location of old cemeteries, rock formations, and such, but it's even more appealing to just explore the smaller trails on your own and discover pretty, peaceful Mackinac. Everything's well marked, and you can't really get lost anyway—you're on a small island, after all.

ACCOMMODATIONS

Along with the 🄲 **Grand Hotel** (286 Grand Ave., 906/847-3331 or 800/334-7263, www.grandhotel.com, $275-805 d), there are plenty of grand and graceful places to stay on Mackinac Island. Yes, rates can be high, but don't dismiss staying on Mackinac; you can find reasonable rates at smaller B&Bs and apartments, the latter of which often have good deals for weeklong stays. The options here tip both ends of the scale.

The venerable **Chippewa Hotel Waterfront** (7221-103 Main St., 906/847-3341 or 866/847-6575, www.chippewahotel.com, $100-575 d) is a classy and comfortable place to stay, with a location in the heart of the island, overlooking the marina. The 24-person lakeside hot

NORTHEAST MICHIGAN

MACKINAC'S MIGRANT VISITORS

While the Straits of Mackinac usually serve as a mighty barrier for many of the mammals that dwell on Mackinac Island, Michigan winters can indeed alter the situation, allowing some of the larger mammals, such as wolves, bears, and deer, to reach the mainland via an ice bridge. So, unlike the isolated isles of warmer climates, this 2,200-acre island is less of a biological vacuum. In fact, many of its seasonal visitors are migrant birds, who use this popular migration spot as a resort habitat in the spring, while en route to summer homes in the north.

Although Mackinac Island also attracts seasonal recreationists, such as hikers and bikers, bird-watchers are especially fond of this enchanted place. In late April and early May, you'll spot golden eagles, bald eagles, red-tailed hawks, and broad-winged hawks flying above. Yellow warblers, American redstarts, and indigo buntings arrive in summer. Along the shoreline, you might also see herrings, cormorants, great blue herons, loons, and Canadian geese. Even wintertime guests will be treated to bird sightings: Beautiful snowy owls and great gray owls often fly south from the Arctic to savor the comparatively warmer climate of Mackinac Island.

Of course, some bird species stay here year-round, including cardinals, blue jays, black-capped chickadees, and large red-crested woodpeckers. The difference between them and many other native inhabitants is that they're here by choice. They can spread their wings and leave at any time – unlike coyotes, for instance, which must wait for an ice bridge to form before making their escape.

tub alone may be worth the stay. Meanwhile, the **Hotel Iroquois** (7485 Main St., 906/847-3321, www.iroquoishotel.com, $215-495 d, suites $395-1,075) offers 46 well-appointed guest rooms and suites, including the two-bedroom Lighthouse Suite, which features spectacular views of Round Island Light. Besides private baths, cable television, and complimentary wireless Internet service, this lovely hotel provides direct access to a private sunbathing beach as well as the Carriage House, one of the island's finest restaurants.

The **Mission Point Resort** (6633 Main St., 906/847-3312 or 800/833-7711, www.missionpoint.com, $149-599 d) may have Mackinac's very best location, spread across 18 acres at the island's southeastern tip. Though not from the Victorian era—it was built in the 1950s by the Moral Rearmament Movement, a post-World War II patriotic group—the sprawling, bright-white resort is attractive and well maintained, with beautiful lawns lined with Adirondack chairs. Amenities include an outdoor pool, tennis and volleyball courts, and loads of children's activities.

From May through October, visitors can opt for a stay at the unique **Jacob Wendell House Bed & Breakfast** (231/818-0334, www.jacobwendellhouse.com, $89-295 d), situated on Main Street, within walking distance of the downtown shopping area and marina. Built in 1846, this picturesque, Federal-style B&B offers four lovely bedrooms, each of which features a full private bath, plus access to a spacious living room, a formal dining room, and a comfortable kitchen.

If you're looking for a more economical place to stay on the island, the year-round **Pontiac Lodge** (1346 Hoban St., 906/847-3364, www.pontiaclodge.com, $65-180 d) features 10 simply furnished rooms as well as three apartments, ideal for families. Conveniently situated near the ferry dock, this comfortable hotel also boasts an on-site eatery, the Village Inn Restaurant.

FOOD

One of the best dining deals on the island is the ◖ **Fort Mackinac Tea Room** (906/847-3328, www.grandhotel.com, 11am-3pm daily June-Sept., $8-14), located in the lower level of the Officers' Stone Quarters within the fort.

Surrounded by thick masonry walls, the tea room serves up both a great atmosphere and delicious food, with good soups, salads, and sandwiches prepared by Grand Hotel chefs. Opt for a spot on the terrace since the high setting is outstanding, and forts were not exactly designed for expansive views.

Of course, everyone has to hit the **Pink Pony** (7221-103 Main St., 906/847-3341, www. chippewahotel.com, 8am-1:30am daily, $7-34) at least sometime during a Mackinac visit. Located in the Chippewa Hotel overlooking the marina, this is *the* party place following the famed Chicago-to-Mac yacht race. The food's terrific, too, with various omelets for breakfast, yummy salads and sandwiches on the lunch menu, and steaks, seafood, and ribs for dinner.

Another tasty downtown option is **The Yankee Rebel Tavern** (1493 Astor St., 906/847-6249, www.yankeerebeltavern.com, 10:30am-midnight daily, $14-32), which serves American-style comfort food, from traditional pot roast to pistachio-encrusted whitefish. Named after the famous underdog horse from 1938, the nearby **Seabiscuit Café** (906/847-3611, www.seabiscuitcafe.com, 10am-2am daily Apr.-Oct., $10-22) prepares some colorfully named appetizers, such as the Painted Pony Macaroni or the War Admiral Hot Wings, plus various salads, sandwiches, and heartier meals, ranging from curry chicken to baby back ribs.

Sooner or later, however, you'll succumb to fudge, a visitor treat since Victorian tourism days. In fact, fudge shops pepper the downtown shopping area. One of the oldest, **Murdick's Fudge** (7363 Main St., 906/847-3530, www. originalmurdicksfudge.com), established in 1887, has a prime Main Street location, where you can buy a sizable slab to take or mail home, or just a small sliver to nibble during your downtown stroll. After all, a little bit goes a long way.

INFORMATION AND SERVICES

For more information about Mackinac Island, contact the helpful **Mackinac Island Tourism**

Bureau (7274 Main St., 877/847-0086, www. mackinacisland.org, 9am-5pm daily), which is located across from the Arnold Transit ferry dock. For further information, consult www. mackinac.com or pick up a copy of the weekly *Mackinac Island Town Crier* (www.mackinacislandnews.com).

Mackinac Island offers a limited amount of services, including a couple of groceries, one post office, and a small police department. For banking needs, stop by the **Central Savings Bank** (21 Hoban St., 906/847-3759, www. centralsavingsbank.com). In case of a medical emergency, dial **911** from any phone or consult the **Mackinac Island Medical Center** (906/847-3582, www.mackinacstraitshealth.org), which offers an on-call staff 24 hours daily.

GETTING THERE AND AROUND
Getting There

More than a million people visit Mackinac Island every year, so getting here isn't a problem. One option is to fly into **Pellston Regional Airport** (PLN, 1395 US-31, Pellston, 231/539-8441 or 231/539-8442, www.pellstonairport. com), then either charter a flight to the island through **Great Lakes Air, Inc.** (906/643-7165, www.greatlakesair.net, one-way $28 adults, $14 children 4-12, children under 4 free) or use the **Mackinaw Shuttle** (231/539-7005 or 888/349-8294, www.mackinawshuttle.com) to reach the ferry docks in Mackinaw City or St. Ignace. If you're coming from somewhere else in Michigan, you can also reach the ferry docks by private vehicle.

No matter what, though, you'll find that there are in fact three ferry services that can zip you across the Straits of Mackinac in less than 20 minutes: the **Arnold Transit Co.** (906/847-3351 or 800/542-8528, www.arnoldline.com, round-trip $23 adults, $12 children 5-12, children under 5 free, $8 bikes), **Shepler's Mackinac Island Ferry** (231/436-5023, 906/643-9440, or 800/828-6157, www. sheplersferry.com, late Apr.-Oct., round-trip $25 adults, $13 children 5-12, children under 5 free, $8 bikes), and **Star Line** (800/638-9892,

biking on Mackinac Island

www.mackinacferry.com, round-trip $25 adults, $13 children 5-12, children under 5 free, $8 bikes).

During the main tourist season—May-October—they operate several times daily. Only one, the longstanding Arnold Transit, in operation since 1878, offers service November-April (from St. Ignace only). Since much of the island shuts down for the winter, you'll find it a little more challenging to reach Mackinac between December and March.

No matter which ferry you choose, it will deposit you at the southern end of the island, in the heart of the hotels and shops lining Main

Street, which follows the curve of the waterfront. It's a wild scene: Dock workers load luggage onto pull-carts and carriages, flocks of bikers dodge horse-drawn buggies, and pedestrians stream up and down the road eating fudge and window-shopping.

Getting Around

Navigating Mackinac Island isn't tough, though you'll have to do it without a motorized vehicle. Cars, after all, aren't allowed on the island. Instead, you can rely on horse-drawn "taxis," which are available from **Mackinac Island Carriage Tours** (906/847-3323 or 906/847-3307, www.mict.com, $4.75-7.25 pp) 24 hours daily during the summer months; November-April, such services are available by appointment. If you enjoy walking and hiking, however, you can easily traverse Mackinac on foot; in fact, it's a wonderfully scenic place for casual strolls and all-day hikes.

The island is also a terrific locale for biking. Bike rentals are available all over downtown; the **Mackinac Island Bike Shop** (906/847-6337, www.bikemackinac.com), for instance, rents mountain bikes, cruisers, tandems, and tag-a-longs for $7-12 hourly or $30-70 daily. All bikes are available in men's and women's styles, and kids' bikes are available, too. It's also possible to rent pet carriers, strollers, and wheelchairs. Equipment varies greatly, though, so look before you pay. Of course, if you plan to do much biking, you'll likely be happier with your own bike, since you can transport it on the ferry. Just remember that you'll want a hybrid or mountain bike to negotiate most interior trails, and be sure to bring your own helmet.

Cheboygan and Vicinity

With a population of 4,800, Cheboygan ranks as one of the largest cities along Lake Huron. While the town offers history buffs a few interesting sites, including a 19th-century opera house, it mainly appeals to outdoor enthusiasts, who venture beyond the city limits to explore surrounding lakes, rivers, and forests. Boaters and anglers especially focus their gaze inland, where a 45-mile-long waterway links Lake Huron with several large inland lakes, ending just shy of Lake Michigan's Little Traverse Bay. Cheboygan sits at the mouth of this popular waterway, welcoming boaters with open arms. Hikers, bird-watchers, and other lovers of the outdoors will find plenty to interest them here, too.

SIGHTS
Historic Sites and Lighthouses

The **Cheboygan History Center** (427 Court St., 231/627-9597, www.cheboyganhistorycenter.org, 1pm-4pm Tues.-Sat. Memorial Day-Sept., $2 pp) was built in 1882 and served as the county jail and local sheriff's home until 1969. The two-story brick structure houses a parlor, kitchen, schoolroom, and bedroom in period style, with an adjacent building that contains logging and marine displays.

The city's **Opera House** (403 N. Huron, 231/627-5841, www.theoperahouse.org, 10am-4pm daily, $2) once entertained the likes of Mary Pickford and Annie Oakley. Built in 1877 and later rebuilt after an 1888 fire, the Victorian-style theater serves as a stage for local entertainment and is open for tours in summer.

From the boardwalk in **Gordon Turner Park** at the northern end of Huron Street, you can gaze out over one of the largest cattail marshes in the Great Lakes. A nesting ground for more than 50 species, it's a favorite of bird-watchers. From the boardwalk and nearby fisherman's walkway, you also can see the Mackinac Bridge as well as Round and Bois Blanc Islands. Visitors might also appreciate the quaint 1884

Cheboygan Crib Light, an octagonal structure that, when deactivated, was relocated from the mouth of the Cheboygan River to the base of the west breakwater on Lake Huron. Now, the pretty white-and-red lighthouse is an ideal stop for photographers.

Parks and Preserves

Cheboygan's **Grass Bay Preserve** contains a rare find in the Great Lakes—one of the finest examples of an original interdunal wetland habitat, characterized by beach pools, marshes, flats, and wetlands, all separated by low dunes. Owned by The Nature Conservancy, this delicate ecosystem comprises a great diversity of plants, including more than 25 species of orchids and 11 types of conifers. Four of the species—dwarf lake iris, Lake Huron tansy, Pitcher's thistle, and Houghton's goldenrod—grow only on the Lake Huron and Lake Michigan shores.

The Nature Conservancy considers Grass Bay its best property in Michigan. The preserve's original 80 acres have grown to more than 830, including a one-mile stretch of Lake Huron shore. From May to September, Grass Bay is noted for its carpet of wildflowers, including lady's slipper, Indian paintbrush, blue harebell, and sundews. The best way to take them all in is from one of the park's two short trails, which wander through an aspen/birch forest and across old shoreline ridges to the beach. Note, however, that this is private—and very fragile—land. Parking can be hard to find, too—most visitors use lots on US-23 (ask first). For more information, contact **The Nature Conservancy** (517/316-0300, www.nature.org)

RECREATION

For hikers and cross-country skiers, the **Wildwood Hills Pathway** on Wildwood Road in nearby Indian River offers almost complete isolation. Three well-marked trails—ranging

NORTHEAST MICHIGAN

4-9 miles in length—take visitors deep into the heart of a northern Michigan second-growth forest and cross high, rolling hills in the Mackinac State Forest just a few miles south of Burt Lake.

Two trailheads on Wildwood Road provide access to the pathway, leading into a dense forest of hardwoods and evergreens. Along the way, the only companion you'll likely have is the wind through the trees, an occasional bird-call, and a curious chipmunk or two. Trail system maps are located at the trailheads and most major intersections.

The swift and turbulent Pigeon River, designated by the state as a natural river, is the highlight of the **Agnes S. Andreae Nature Preserve**. Located in Indian River, the beautifully secluded 27-acre preserve includes 2,000 feet of Pigeon River frontage. On the river's west side, a lowland stand of cedar bordering the riverbank rises to high bluffs covered with conifers and dense hardwoods. There are no designated trails, but hikers and cross-country skiers find well-worn tracks to follow and other trails that border the river. Like many other tracts in this undeveloped part of the state, the preserve is owned by the **Little Traverse Conservancy** (3264 Powell Rd., Harbor Springs, 231/347-0991, www.landtrust.org).

ACCOMMODATIONS AND FOOD

There are several decent motels in the Cheboygan area, such as the **Best Western River Terrace Motel** (847 S. Main St., 231/627-5688, www.bestwesternmichigan.com, $143-169 d), with most rooms overlooking the Cheboygan River. You can also camp at **Cheboygan State Park** (4490 Beach Rd., 616/627-2811, annual $11 Recreation Passport for Michigan residents or $8.40 day-use fee/$30.50 yearly Recreation Passport for non-residents required), at one of 78 modern sites ($12-27 daily) along Lake Huron's Duncan Bay. The area is a favorite among anglers, but there's not much in the way of swimming at the campground; instead, head for the park's

day-use area, four miles away, which has a sandy beach and bathhouse.

For good food served up with interesting history, try the **Hack-Ma-Tack Inn & Restaurant** (8131 Beebe Rd., 231/625-2919, www.hackmatackinn.com, 5pm-10pm daily May-mid-Oct., $18-50), housed in a rustic 1894 lodge overlooking the Cheboygan River. Whitefish is the specialty.

INFORMATION AND SERVICES

For more information about Cheboygan, contact the **Cheboygan Area Chamber of Commerce** (124 N. Main St., 231/627-7183, www.cheboygan.com, 9am-5pm Mon.-Fri.). For local news and events, consult the *Cheboygan Daily Tribune* (www.cheboygannews.com).

Cheboygan offers most of the services that travelers might require. Here, you'll find groceries, banks, even a **post office** (200 N. Main St., 231/627-9898, www.usps.com). In case of a police-related or medical emergency, dial **911** from any phone. For medical assistance, visit the **Cheboygan Memorial Hospital** (748 S. Main St., 231/627-5601, www.cheboyganhospital.org).

GETTING THERE AND AROUND

From **Pellston Regional Airport** (PLN, 1395 US-31, Pellston, 231/539-8441 or 231/539-8442, www.pellstonairport.com), you can rent a car, head north on US-31, and take CR-66 east to Cheboygan. Without traffic, the 20-mile trip should take about 24 minutes. As an alternative, you can take a bus directly to Cheboygan (309 E. State St.) via **Greyhound** (800/231-2222, www.greyhound.com) or **Indian Trails** (800/292-3831, www.indian-trails.com).

Of course, if you're already traversing Michigan by car, you can reach Cheboygan via several convenient routes, including M-27, M-33, or US-23. From Sault Ste. Marie, for instance, simply merge onto I-75 South, cross the

Mackinac Bridge (for which you'll have to pay a toll), and continue onto US-23 South to downtown Cheboygan, a 74-mile trip that usually takes about 80 minutes. From Traverse City, meanwhile, you can take M-72 East to US-131 North, continue onto CR-42 and M-32 East, merge onto I-75 North, and follow Levering Road to Cheboygan, a 114-mile trip that normally takes about two hours. Even downtown Detroit is only four hours away; simply follow I-375 North to I-75 North, continue north for 275 miles, and take Levering Road to Cheboygan—a journey that, in all, will cover about 284 miles. Then, once in Cheboygan, you can easily get around via car, bike, or foot.

THE INLAND WATERWAY

The geography of this region was kind to the early Indians and French voyageurs traversing the Lower Peninsula: A chain of lakes and rivers forms a 45-mile water route, very nearly linking Lakes Michigan and Huron. The route was safer and faster than traveling on the big lakes, and certainly beat the heck out of portaging. Today, the inland waterway remains extremely popular, mostly for fishing and recreational boating. Narrower portions are dredged to a depth of five feet and a width of 30 feet. Boats up to 30 feet long can join in on what sometimes looks like a nautical parade.

Burt Lake State Park

Big Burt Lake is the focus of its namesake **state park** (6635 State Dr., Indian River, 231/238-9392, annual $11 Recreation Passport for Michigan residents or $8.40 day-use fee/$30.50 yearly Recreation Passport for nonresidents required), located at the lake's southern end. Anglers flock to this 10-mile-long lake, known as one of the best fisheries in the state for walleye, panfish, and bass—but especially walleye. Swimmers seek it out, too, since a soft sand beach runs the entire length of the park. The park has two boat launches, one located next to

a popular campground with 375 modern sites ($22 daily). The park offers little in the way of hiking, but does have a nifty observation tower that gives you a great view of the lake.

Mullett Lake

Popular with anglers, Mullett Lake also has a lesser-known claim to fame: the origin of the term *kemosabe*, used by Tonto in *The Lone Ranger*. Yep, it's true—according to the die-hard research of Cecil Adams, anyway, who authors "The Straight Dope," a quirky fact-finding column that began in the *Chicago Reader* and has appeared in alternative weeklies around the country.

Adams's research revealed that the word *kemosabe* appears to have originated with Jim Jewell, a director for *The Lone Ranger*. Jewell had stated in an interview that he took the term from Kamp Kee-Mo-Sah-Bee, a boys' camp in Mackinac, Michigan. According to Jewell, *kee-mo-sah-bee* translates to "trusty scout."

Speaking of name mysteries, no one really knows why a small town on the east end of Mullett Lake was originally named Aloha Depot. Today, it's the site of **Aloha State Park** (231/625-2522, annual $11 Recreation Passport for Michigan residents or $8.40 day-use fee/$30.50 yearly Recreation Passport for nonresidents required), a small 100-acre state park that primarily consists of a boat launch and 295-site campground ($14 daily). Not particularly picturesque by Michigan standards, most sites sit in a relatively open setting, with just a handful directly on the water.

Along with neighboring Burt Lake, pretty Mullett Lake is one of the most popular and productive fishing lakes in the state. Anglers vie for walleye and northern pike, but larger stuff lurks down there as well: In 1974, Mullett produced a 193-pound sturgeon, a scaly, long-nosed creature that hasn't evolved much since prehistoric times. Think about that while you're taking a dip.

Rogers City to Alpena

Driving along the picturesque Lake Huron shore, you'll encounter several slow-moving communities, including Rogers City, home to lovely lighthouses, parks, and beaches, and Alpena, a larger city favored by outdoor enthusiasts for its wildlife sanctuary and underwater preserve.

Despite its beautiful beaches, few travelers visit Rogers City, a quiet town of about 2,800, better known as home to the world's largest limestone quarry. The Huron shore's limestone was formed by ancient seas that once covered most of the state. Full of coral-forming organisms, they eventually created large limestone deposits, one of which nears the earth's surface in Rogers City. In 1907, tests found that the limestone was unusually pure, ideal for making steel and many chemicals. The Michigan Limestone and Chemical Company was formed a year later, and subsequently purchased by U.S. Steel. Nearly four miles long and roughly three miles wide, the quarry is expected to produce well into the 21st century.

Alpena, protected by the deep curve of Thunder Bay, is the largest city north of Bay City on the Lake Huron shore, yet has always been tinged by a lack of respect. When surveyed in 1839, a deed to the land was offered to anyone in the survey party in lieu of summer wages, but few took the offer. At the time, the area was considered mostly a desolate cedar swamp.

Not long after, however, the intrepid Daniel Carter arrived with his wife and young daughter and built a log cabin, becoming the town's first white settler. By 1857, a store and boardinghouse had popped up, and in 1859, Alpena became the site of the county's first steam-powered sawmill. Before long, some 20 lumber and shingle mills buzzed life into the growing town.

Today, the town's economy relies on a large cement industry. But for visitors, it also offers the chance to enjoy the natural beauty of the Great Lakes without the trendy development and gentrification that have taken over so many of the old resort towns on the opposite side of the state.

Part of the reason visitors have overlooked Alpena is because it's not that easy to reach. More than 70 miles from the nearest interstate, it remains an unpretentious working-class town of corner bars and friendly residents. For decades, diversified industries, including paper mills, cement plants, and an Air Force base, meant that the area didn't have to seek out the tourist trade the way other areas have.

But with its bread-and-butter industries gone, Alpena has learned to promote its assets. And there's plenty worth promoting, including two lightly visited state parks with several miles of Lake Huron shoreline, a handsome marina, an impressive museum, northern Michigan's only year-round professional theater, and a fascinating underwater preserve with more than 80 shipwrecks.

SIGHTS

Besser Museum for Northeast Michigan

The excellent **Besser Museum for Northeast Michigan** (491 Johnson St., Alpena, 989/356-2202, www.bessermuseum.org, 10am-5pm daily, $5 adults, $3 children) combines art, history, and science on two levels. The museum's highlight is the "Gallery of Early Man," a collection of Great Lakes Native American artifacts considered one of the finest in the country. To the probable dismay of archaeologists, the collection, which numbers more than 60,000 pieces, was gathered by Gerald Haltiner, a local state highway worker, and his museum-curator son, Robert.

The museum purchased the collection from the Haltiners in the 1970s and is working closely with local Native American tribes to review the collection with repatriation in mind. Some of its most intriguing artifacts are the copper items that date back more than 7,000

© DANIEL MARTONE

Alpena's Besser Museum for Northeast Michigan

years, made by a people known only as the Copper Culture. The museum's Sky Theater Planetarium puts on changing shows, many with Native American themes, throughout the year.

Alpena Wildlife Sanctuary

Alpena Wildlife Sanctuary (Wildlife Sanctuary Board, 989/595-3919 or 989/354-1770, www.alpena.mi.us), on US-23 within the Alpena city limits, has been a favorite sanctuary of hikers, paddlers, anglers, and nature lovers since it was established in 1938 by the Michigan Conservation Department. The 500-acre refuge bordering the Thunder Bay River contains a large expanse of wetlands, an island with fishing platforms, and a viewing platform that overlooks the river. According to the Thunder Bay Audubon Society, more than 130 different species of birds have been spotted here. Year-round residents include Canada geese and mute swans; spring migration brings others, including buffleheads, canvasbacks, whistling swans, and more.

Lighthouses

Travelers who find the Huron shore lacking in comparison with the state's Lake Michigan shore change their minds after a visit to the **40 Mile Point Lighthouse.** Seven miles north of Rogers City on US-23, a limitless expanse of blue water sweeps in a 180-degree arc to the horizon. A gently sloping beach proves just right for wading, sandcastle building, and swimming. The 52-foot-tall lighthouse, built in 1897, stands guard as a reminder that Huron can, and does, turn dangerous. Though not open to the public, it is a favorite of photographers.

Other lighthouses along this stretch include the 1905 **Middle Island Lighthouse** and the 1832 **Thunder Bay Island Light,** both accessible via boat. In Alpena, you won't need a vessel to view the 1914 **Alpena Light,** a skeletal red structure near the Thunder Bay River.

Beaches and Parks

Many rate **P. H. Hoeft State Park** (US-23 N, Rogers City, 989/734-2543, annual $11

NORTHEAST MICHIGAN

© DANIEL MARTONE

the 40 Mile Point Lighthouse near Rogers City

Recreation Passport for Michigan residents or $8.40 day-use fee/$30.50 yearly Recreation Passport for nonresidents required) as the most beautiful state park along Michigan's Lake Huron shore. It's easy to see why. With a mile-long swath of soft, white sand, low rolling dunes, and a mixed hardwood/conifer forest, it offers a breathtaking, simple beauty. Surprisingly, it's also one of the least visited state parks in the Lower Peninsula. Even the 144-site modern campground ($22 daily), set against mature pines and hardwoods with lots of shade and privacy, sits half empty most of the time. Head directly for sites 1-33, located just a few steps from the beach. One cabin and four rent-a-tents are also available.

Behind the park's picnic area lies an almost totally undeveloped area, with dunes and woods that abound in wildlife and vegetation. Naturalists can search for the more than 40 species of wildflowers that grow here, including many orchids and irises rare in the state and North America. More than four miles of trails

loop through the area for hikers and cross-country skiers.

From Rogers City, it's just 11 miles west on M-68 to the Lower Peninsula's only major waterfall. **Ocqueoc (Sacred Water) Falls** cascades over a series of two- to six-foot drops. The picturesque site is a favorite of picnickers, sunbathers, and swimmers. A seven-mile trail for hikers and cross-country skiers starts next to the falls.

Just a few hundred yards away, the **Bicentennial Pathway** (created in 1976) loops through the deep woods and over the gently rolling hills of the Mackinaw State Forest. The pathway's three loops measure 3, 4, and 6.5 miles and are well used by area hikers. Bed down at the **Ocqueoc Falls State Forest Campground,** across M-68.

Just north of Rogers City on US-23, **Seagull Point Park** (193 E. Michigan Ave.) draws visitors to its beautiful beach, curved like a scimitar. A wide band of soft sand and a gradual slope into Lake Huron create a perfect spot for beachcombers, sunbathers, and families. Behind the beach, a two-mile interpretive trail winds through a series of low dunes, with signs along the route that identify the area's natural history and accompanying flora and fauna. Near the park, the **Herman Vogler Conservation Area** (240 W. Erie St., Rogers City, 989/734-4000) provides a quiet, car-free area on the Trout River. Five miles of nature trails are open to cross-country skiing in the winter.

Negwegon State Park (Ossineke, 989/724-5126, annual $11 Recreation Passport for Michigan residents or $8.40 day-use fee/$30.50 yearly Recreation Passport for nonresidents required) is the carefully guarded secret of a number of outdoor lovers. What exactly are they hiding? Some of the most beautiful and most isolated beaches on Lake Huron. The 2,469-acre park's shoreline stretches for more than six miles, a lovely string of bays and coves.

Named after Chippewa chief Negwegon, the park also offers three hiking trails named after Native American tribes: the Algonquin, Chippewa, and Potawatomi. The 10 miles of trails skirt the shoreline and loop through a heavily wooded interior. A serene retreat, this isolated park offers natural beauty to hikers and backpackers willing to trade conveniences for quiet, contemplative walks along 8 miles of Lake Huron shoreline. Note: There are no camping or picnic facilities here.

Between this park and the considerably smaller **Harrisville State Park** (248 State Park Rd., Harrisville, 989/724-5126, annual $11 Recreation Passport for Michigan residents or $8.40 day-use fee/$30.50 yearly Recreation Passport for nonresidents required) is one of several lighthouses along the Lake Huron shore. The gleaming white **Sturgeon Point Lighthouse** (989/727-4703, www.alconahistoricalsociety.com, 11am-4pm Fri.-Sat. Memorial Day-Sept., free), built in 1869, is still active today—as both a lighthouse and a maritime museum. The grounds are open to the public year-round.

◖ DIVING IN THUNDER BAY

Divers have their own sanctuary just off the Alpena shore. Here, the **Thunder Bay National Marine Sanctuary and Underwater Preserve** thrills divers with its clear waters, interesting underwater limestone formations, and shipwrecks. Rocky islands and hazardous shoals proved treacherous for mariners; the preserve protects some 80 shipwrecks, 14 of which can be explored with the help of a wreck-diving charter. Among the most popular are the *Nordmeer,* a German steel steamer that sank in 1966, and the *Montana,* a 235-foot steamer that burned and sank in 1914. **Thunder Bay Scuba** (413 S. Ripley Blvd., Alpena, 989/356-6228, www.tbscuba.com, 9am-5:30pm Mon.-Fri., 10am-2pm Sat.-Sun.) offers charter diving services for about $44 per day, departing from Alpena's city marina.

The state established the Thunder Bay National Marine Sanctuary and Underwater Preserve—more than 288 protected miles in all—in 1981, largely to prohibit divers from removing artifacts from the site. In October 2000, the state preserve was also designated a national marine sanctuary, a status that grants it federal funding and additional resources for scientific and archaeological study. For more information, contact the **Michigan Underwater Preserve Council** (800/970-8717, www.michiganpreserves.org).

ACCOMMODATIONS AND FOOD

Lodging choices are pretty limited in Rogers City. The best place in town (and the only place with an indoor pool) is the 43-room **Driftwood Motel** (540 W. 3rd St., 989/734-4777, $49-99 d), which overlooks Lake Huron. Adjacent to the motel, the **Waters Edge Restaurant** (530 N. 3rd St., 989/734-4747, 11am-10pm daily, $9-23) serves up Lake Huron views and fish dishes.

Hotels and restaurants in Alpena have a funky, nostalgic vibe, as if you've been transported back to the 1950s or 1960s. Chief among them are the **40 Winks Motel** (1021 S. State Ave., 989/354-5622, www.40winksmotel.com, $49-69 d), with simple rooms opposite Lake Huron.

OMER IN THE NEWS

Located along the Sunrise Side Coastal Highway (US-23), Omer is one of the tiniest towns in Michigan. In fact, a sign posted at the city limit even claims that it's "Michigan's smallest city." Founded as a logging town in the mid-1860s and originally called Rifle River Mills, the town was renamed by the first postmaster, who wanted to call it Homer. When, however, he discovered that Michigan already had a town named Homer – southeast of Marshall – he dropped the "H," and the town of Omer was incorporated as a city in the early 20th century.

With a current population of just over 300, Omer has little to recommend it to travelers – except, perhaps, its proximity to the Rifle River. Still, the town is curious for at least one other reason. It was near here that, in August 1998, Timothy Joseph Boomer, a 24-year-old engineer, was canoeing with friends when he fell into the water and began yelling a long string of expletives in the presence of a man, his wife, and their two young children. A sheriff's deputy, who heard the shouts downstream, ticketed Boomer for violating an 1897 law that claimed anyone using immoral or obscene language within earshot of a woman or child could be charged with a misdemeanor. An Arenac County jury found Boomer guilty of the charge, and though a district judge ruled the ban on cursing in front of women unconstitutional, he left intact the provision concerning children. Boomer was fined $75 and ordered to work in a child-care program, but the sentence was postponed during the appeals process.

The case of the "cussing canoeist" sparked a nationwide debate about free speech and public behavior. While some protested the vague nature of the law – which could leave the question of what constitutes "indecent" language up for interpretation – others defended the need to regulate improper conduct, especially in front of children. Needless to say, the American Civil Liberties Union (ACLU) was only too quick to handle the case, and in 2002, the Michigan Court of Appeals successfully overturned the 105-year-old law. Afterward, the "cussing canoeist," who had initially admitted to using only a few choice words (not the alleged string of them), decided to be more careful about what he said in public.

INFORMATION AND SERVICES

For more information about this area, contact the **Rogers City Chamber of Commerce** (292 S. Bradley Hwy., Rogers City, 989/734-2535, www.rogerscity.com) or the **Alpena Area Convention & Visitors Bureau** (235 W. Chisholm St., Alpena, 800/425-7362, www.alpenacvb.com). For local news, consult the *Presque Isle County Advance* (www.piadvance.com) or the *Alpena News* (www.thealpenanews.com).

Between Rogers City and Alpena, you're likely to find the services you need, from groceries and pharmacies to banks and post offices. In case of a medical emergency, dial **911** from any phone or consult **Alpena Regional Medical Center** (1501 W. Chisholm St.,

Alpena, 989/356-7000, www.alpenaregionalmedicalcenter.org).

GETTING THERE AND AROUND

To reach Alpena, some travelers may choose to fly; luckily, Delta Air Lines offers commuter service to the **Alpena County Regional Airport** (APN, 1617 Airport Rd., Alpena, 989/354-2907, www.alpenaairport.com), where you can either hail a cab or rent a car. From there, you can then drive (or be driven) to Rogers City by taking M-32 West, M-65 North, and US-23 North to West Erie Street, a 37-mile trip that will usually take about 44 minutes. As an alternative, you can ride a bus to this part of northeastern Michigan; after all, both **Greyhound** (989/734-4903 or 800/231-2222, www.greyhound.com) and **Indian Trails**

(800/292-3831, www.indiantrails.com) provide service to Rogers City (285 S. Bradley) as well as Alpena (1141 N. US-23).

Of course, it's probably easier (and cheaper) to reach this area via car. From I-75, take M-68 to Rogers City or M-32 to Alpena. Both towns can also be accessed via US-23 along the coast. To get an idea of how long it might take to reach this area, consider the trip between Sault Ste. Marie and Rogers City: From the Soo, you'll take I-75 South, cross the Mackinac Bridge (a toll bridge), merge onto US-23 South, and continue on the Sunrise Side Coastal Highway (US-23) to Rogers City, a 115-mile trip that typically takes about two hours. From Traverse City, meanwhile, you can take M-72 East to M-66 North/US-131 North, continue onto Mancelona Road and Old State Road, follow Meridian Line Road for 4 miles, and then take M-32 East to Alpena, a 128-mile trip that will usually take 2.5 hours. You can also access this area from downtown Detroit by taking I-375 North to I-75 North, merging onto US-23 North, and following the Sunrise Side Coastal Highway to Alpena; without traffic, the 243-mile trip should take less than four hours. No matter how you reach these two coastal towns, though, you can easily get around via car, bike, or foot.

PRESQUE ISLE

It would be easy to pass the Presque Isle peninsula and never know it was there. Easy, but a mistake. This almost completely undiscovered resort area off the beaten path between Rogers City and Alpena features two of the jewels in the region's crown. Both are well worth driving out of the way to see.

On a map, the peninsula looks like a beckoning finger (*presqu'île* means "peninsula"—"almost an island"—in French). Two classic lighthouses perch at the tip of the strangely shaped peninsula, including the tallest lighthouse on the Great Lakes.

Inside the **Old Presque Isle Lighthouse complex** (5295 E. Grand Lake Rd., 989/595-6979 or 989/595-5419, www.presqueislelighthouses.org, 9am-6pm daily May-Oct., free), which consists of a light tower and a nearby keeper's dwelling, exhibits and displays relate the history of Great Lakes shipping and light keeping. Artifacts and antiques that range from wooden doors from a shipwreck to an old pump organ that visitors can play. Built in 1840, the lighthouse was used for 30 years until it was replaced by a new light a mile north. But no automatic light can provide the view you'll get from the parapet surrounding the lantern room, reached by a trip up the two-story tower's winding steps.

The **New Presque Isle Lighthouse and Museum** (4500 E. Grand Lake Rd., 989/595-5419 or 989/595-9917, www.presqueislelighthouses.org, 9am-6pm daily May-Oct., free) dates to 1870. Trees had grown to obscure the older, shorter lighthouse; the "new" one stretches to 113 feet, the tallest on all the Great Lakes. Situated in the middle of 100-acre **Presque Isle Lighthouse Park,** the tower and restored light keeper's house look much as they did more than a century ago. Inside, a caretaker—a descendant of generations of

the New Presque Isle Lighthouse and Museum

Great Lakes sailors—plays the part of a turn-of-the-20th-century light keeper on special occasions.

The park's fine nature trails begin at the lighthouse and circle the peninsula's tip. The trails border rugged shoreline, then weave in and out of evergreens and hardwoods, before reaching the peninsula's tip and a sweeping view of Lake Huron from a rocky beach.

Besser Natural Area, now part of **Rockport State Recreation Area** (annual $11 Recreation Passport for Michigan residents or $8.40 day use fee/$30.50 yearly Recreation Passport for nonresidents required), offers an intriguing mix of attractions: nearly a mile of wild, undeveloped Lake Huron shoreline, a ghost town, a sunken ship, and one of the few remaining stands of virgin white pine left in the state.

Reach the 134-acre preserve by taking Grand Lake Road six miles southeast of Presque Isle. For more information, contact **Harrisville State Park** (989/724-5126).

The boom-and-bust logging industry both created and destroyed the ghost town of Bell, which once included a school, a sawmill, a store, a saloon, and several houses during the 1880s. A one-mile self-guided trail leads through a magnificent stand of virgin white pine and passes the ghost town and a tiny inland lagoon, the graveyard for an unnamed small vessel. Halfway along the trail, a plaque honors Jesse Besser, who donated this land to the state in 1966 as a memorial to Michigan's lumbermen. The trail continues through a dark cedar forest before emerging on Lake Huron's shore.

Oscoda to West Branch

Farther along the Lake Huron shore, several towns serve as gateways to incredible outdoor delights, including Oscoda, popular among canoeists, and Tawas City, a favorite among bird-watchers.

Oscoda sits at the mouth of the Au Sable River, famed as a trout stream and navigable by canoe as far as Grayling and Roscommon. The waterway played a prominent part in the state's early pine-logging days. At its most populous, the city's population numbered more than 23,000, and the river was filled with pine logs on their way to the sawmills. While the logs were plentiful, Oscoda grew unchecked. With the depletion of the resource, though, its population began to shrink. Finally, nature put an abrupt end to the city's logging boom: A forest fire swept through in 1911, reducing the city's heyday to ashes. The current population is roughly 900.

As for Tawas City, its name derives from Otawas, the name of an important Chippewa chief. He's honored in this stretch of Lake Huron shore many times over. The twin cities of Tawas City and East Tawas straddle the

Tawas River, which empties into Tawas Bay, formed by a crooked finger of land called—you guessed it—Tawas Point.

Today, local festivals, such as February's Perchville U.S.A., reveal the area's popularity with anglers. Visitors can watch the boat-filled bay in Tawas Point State Park, which occupies the fishhook-shaped Tawas Point. It's a favorite of naturalists, as much for the ever-changing landscape created by wind and waves during annual winter storms as for some of the best bird-watching in the state.

West of Tawas City, West Branch is a small town with quaint Victorian-style architecture, a downtown shopping district, and an outlet mall. It's also not far from a popular recreation area, the Huron National Forest, and the road to Houghton and Higgins Lakes.

SIGHTS
Beaches and Parks

Opposite the large beach on the shore of Tawas Bay, part of 183-acre **Tawas Point State Park** (686 Tawas Beach Rd., East Tawas, 989/362-5041, daily, annual $11 Recreation Passport for

Michigan residents or $8.40 day-use fee/$30.50 yearly Recreation Passport for nonresidents required), the white Victorian-style 1876 **Tawas Point Lighthouse** is undoubtedly the park's most-photographed feature and a favorite among lovers of these classic lights. One of the state's most well-maintained lighthouses, it is often open to the public for self-guided tours. Not far away, bird-watchers gather at the day-use area and nature trail. A checklist of birds spotted in the park lists more than 250, with 31 species of warblers and 17 species of waterfowl.

In summer, swimmers favor this park for its white sand and warm, shallow waters. Anglers and hikers appreciate Tawas Point, too. Here, you'll also find a playground, a picnic area, public restrooms, a spacious campground, and gorgeous sunsets.

From the state park, history buffs can take a self-guided 68-mile driving tour amid key historical, natural, and cultural features west of the park, including the site of a 1984 forest fire, a 1,000-acre marsh that nurtures deer and other wildlife, the 1917 Foote Dam, a former Air Force base, and the Lumberman's Monument, a bronze statue erected in 1931 on the high scenic banks of the Au Sable River. Dedicated to the pioneer spirit and efforts of Michigan lumbermen, the monument isn't far from a visitors center, whose exhibits relate to Michigan's logging era. For more information, pick up brochures at the park office. Here, you can also learn more about the **Highbanks Trail,** a seven-mile, ungroomed route about 14 miles west of Oscoda that traces the bluffs along the southern shore of the Au Sable River and offers scenic views of the popular canoeing waterway and surrounding wildlife. This hiking trail, which is free to utilize and favored by cross-country skiers in winter also provides access to sites like the 14-foot-tall Lumberman's Monument and the Canoer's Memorial, which was erected in 1950 to honor marathon canoe racing.

Rifle River Recreation Area

Inner tubes seem to be the transportation option of choice on the slower-moving Rifle River, which meanders from the **Rifle River Recreation Area** (2550 E. Rose City Rd., Lupton, 989/473-2258, annual $11 Recreation Passport for Michigan residents or $8.40 day use fee/$30.50 yearly Recreation Passport for nonresidents required), about 15 miles northeast of West Branch, to Saginaw Bay, some 90 miles south. Paddlers shouldn't overlook the Rifle, though, since it flows through Devoe Lake, one of five paddle-only lakes in this spacious preserve.

The 4,449 acres that now make up the Rifle River Recreation Area were once part of the private hunting preserve of H. M. Jewett, an early auto-industry tycoon. Today, most of the visitors who are hoping to leave with a catch are bagging bass and other varieties of fish, not four-legged game.

The recreation area includes several miles of paved and packed-dirt trails that travel across one-lane bridges, past forest-fringed lakes, and up several high hills that reveal vistas of tangled stands of cedar. For a great view, head for **Ridge Road,** a dirt track that passes over the park's highest elevations. Those who like to hike can follow 14 miles of picturesque trails that cut through some of the park's most breathtaking terrain.

Visitors can stay at a choice of on-site accommodations, including both rustic and modern campsites as well as five "frontier-style" cabins, all located in secluded areas far from campgrounds and day-trippers. The cabins have vault toilets, hand pumps, and only basic furnishings. In winter, the park is a popular spot for cross-country skiing, ice fishing, and snowmobiling.

SHOPPING

Needless to say, shopping isn't why most people come to the southern reaches of Northeast Michigan. But not all the attractions in this area are of the natural kind. In a seemingly unlikely place, the **Tanger Outlets Center** (2990 Cook Rd., West Branch, 989/345-2594, www.tangeroutlet.com, 9am-9pm Mon.-Sat., 10am-7pm Sun.) offers an enormous variety of mainstream shopping choices, everything from a Gap Outlet to a Bath & Body Works store. The outlet mall lies east of I-75.

C CANOEING ON THE AU SABLE RIVER

While anglers often try their luck on the Au Sable, paddlers may appreciate the river even more. The **AuSable River Canoe Marathon** (www.ausablecanoemarathon.org) starts in Grayling and ends in Oscoda. For canoe rentals, try **Oscoda Canoe Rental** (678 W. River Rd., 989/739-9040, www.oscodacanoe.com, 8am-4pm daily, $25-45 pp) or **Hunt's Canoes & Miniature Golf** (711 Lake St., Oscoda, 989/739-4408, www.huntscanoes.com, $18-40 pp).

Trips on the *Au Sable River Queen* (1775 W. River Rd., Oscoda, 989/739-7351, www.ausableriverqueen.net, 10am-5pm daily, $14 pp) depart from Foote Dam daily in season. The tours are especially popular during fall color, and reservations are recommended.

ACCOMMODATIONS AND FOOD

The **Redwood Motor Lodge** (3111 N. US-23, Oscoda, 989/739-2021, $54-127 d) offers standard motel rooms and cottages near Lake Huron. Also on Lake Huron, the **Rest-All Inn** (4270 N. US-23, Oscoda, 989/739-8822, www.restallinnoscoda.com, $59-109 d) has clean motel rooms (some with microwaves and refrigerators), a beach, and a playground.

In West Branch, stay at the **LogHaven Bed, Breakfast, and Barn** (1550 McGregor Rd., 989/685-3527, www.loghavenbbb.com, $125 d), where you'll find comfortable rooms, private baths, hearty country-style breakfasts, and a place to stable horses. It's a perfect home base for exploring the area's hiking, horseback riding, snowmobiling, and cross-country skiing trails.

Michigan's state parks offer consistently good campgrounds. **Tawas Point State Park** (686 Tawas Beach Rd., East Tawas, 989/362-5041, annual $11 Recreation Passport for Michigan residents or $8.40 day-use fee/$30.50

Paddlers favor the Au Sable River.

yearly Recreation Passport for nonresidents required) is no exception, with 210 campsites ($27 daily) and a large sand beach.

While you won't find any gourmet hideaways in the area, restaurants offer good, stick-to-the-ribs food in generous portions. One good option is **Wiltse's Brew Pub and Family Restaurant** (5606 N. F-41, Oscoda, 989/739-2231, www.wiltsebrewpub.com, 8am-12:30am Mon.-Sat., 8am-9pm Sun., $12-27), where you can order up a homemade brew to wash down the chicken dishes and steaks cut to order.

INFORMATION AND SERVICES

For more information about the area, contact the **Oscoda Area Convention & Visitors Bureau** (P.O. Box 572, Oscoda, MI 48750, 989/739-0900, www.oscoda.com), the **Oscoda-AuSable Chamber of Commerce** (4440 N. US-23, Oscoda, 800/235-4625, www.oscodachamber.com), the **Tawas Bay Tourist & Convention Bureau** (877/868-2927, www.tawasbay.com), the **Tawas Area Chamber of Commerce** (402 E. Lake St., Tawas City, 800/558-2927, www.tawas.com), or the **West Branch-Ogemaw County Travelers & Visitors Bureau** (422 W. Houghton Ave., West Branch, 989/345-2821, www.visitwestbranch.com).

Although you won't find a ton of services in these smaller towns, basics like groceries, banks, and post offices won't be too hard to find. If an emergency occurs, dial **911** or consult **St. Joseph Health System** (200 Hemlock, Tawas City, 800/362-9404, www.sjhsys.org).

GETTING THERE AND AROUND

Despite the relatively remote nature of Oscoda, Tawas City, and West Branch, it's not terribly hard to reach this part of northeastern Michigan. For one thing, you could always fly into the area. Both **Alpena County Regional Airport** (APN, 1617 Airport Rd., Alpena, 989/354-2907, www.alpenaairport.com) and **MBS International Airport** (MBS, 8500 Garfield Rd., Freeland, 989/695-5555, www.mbsairport.org) offer commuter flights via

Delta Air Lines; from both airports, you can then easily rent a car and head to your specific destination. From the Alpena airport, for instance, you can take M-32 East and various surface streets to reach US-23 South, which will lead you directly to Oscoda, a 54-mile trip that usually takes about an hour. From the Freeland airport, meanwhile, you can follow US-10 East to I-75 North, take exit 212, and continue on the I-75 Business Route and M-55 West to West Branch, a 64-mile trip that will typically take about an hour. In addition, both **Greyhound** (800/231-2222, www.greyhound.com) and **Indian Trails** (800/292-3831, www.indiantrails.com) provide bus service to Tawas City (989/362-6120, 1020 W. Lake St.), which is located between West Branch and Oscoda, as well as **Standish** (220 E. Cedar St., 989/846-4613), which lies about 27 miles southeast of West Branch via I-75 and roughly 36 miles southwest of Tawas City via US-23.

Naturally, given the spread-out nature of this region, your best bet will probably be to drive here yourself. From Detroit, for instance, you can reach West Branch by taking I-375 North, merging onto I-75 North, and following the I-75 Business Route and M-55 West into town; without traffic, the 165-mile trip should take about 2.5 hours. Similarly, you can access West Branch from Sault Ste. Marie, via I-75 South, which crosses the Mackinac Bridge (a toll bridge), and M-55 East, a 183-mile trip that, without traffic, will take roughly 2.75 hours. From West Branch, you can then take M-55 East directly to Tawas City, a 37-mile trip that will normally require about 45 minutes, and from Tawas City, you can continue to Oscoda via US-23 North, a 16-mile trip that will usually take about 20 minutes. Once you've arrived in the region, you can get around in a number of ways, including by car, bike, foot, or canoe.

HURON NATIONAL FOREST

Oscoda also is known as the gateway to the **Huron National Forest** (Huron Shores Ranger Station, 5761 N. Skeel Rd., 989/739-0728), which covers most of the acreage between

PADDLING TIPS

Given the bounty of rivers, inland lakes, and coastal waters in and around Michigan, it's no surprise that canoeing and kayaking are popular activities in the Great Lakes State. Options range from short, hour-long canoe trips on the Au Sable River to multiday kayaking journeys around Isle Royale National Park. Though some enthusiasts bring their vessels with them, you can easily rent a variety of canoes and kayaks at several different outfitters, from Ann Arbor to Marquette. In addition, many hotels and resorts offer complimentary canoes and kayaks to their guests.

Paddling throughout Michigan can be a rewarding experience, but it can also be dangerous if you're ill-prepared. High winds and strong currents can make paddling conditions challenging; in fact, while beginners are welcome to give paddling a try, it's helpful if you've had at least some experience before attempting it here. No matter what your experience level, however, the following guidelines are necessary for all canoeists and kayakers to remember:

- Ensure that you've had proper instruction for the vessel that you plan to use.

- Check the daily weather forecast, especially predicted wind speeds, beforehand.

- Be aware of tidal conditions, currents, and water levels; under normal circumstances, you should allow for a minimum paddling time of two miles per hour.

- Inform someone on shore of your plans, especially your intended destination and expected return time; leave a float plan with a responsible individual, place a copy of the plan in a visible spot in your vehicle, and contact the onshore person when you do, in fact, return.

- Arrange to have a vehicle (if not yours) and dry clothes waiting at your take-out point.

- Secure a spare paddle to your vessel.

- Place your keys, identification, money, and other valuables in a waterproof bag and secure the bag to the vessel.

- Apply sunscreen, even on cloudy days, and insect repellent.

- Wear appropriate clothing for weather and water conditions.

- Have a readily accessible, personal flotation device (PFD) with attached whistle for each occupant; children under six must wear PFDs at all times.

- Bring plenty of food and drinking water (one gallon/person/day) in nonbreakable, watertight containers.

- Bring a cell phone in case of an emergency, but don't rely solely on said phone, as reception can be sporadic in the backcountry and offshore waters.

Oscoda to the east and Grayling to the west. Together, the Manistee National Forest in the western part of the state and the Huron National Forest cover more than 950,000 acres in the northern part of the Lower Peninsula. The scenic Au Sable River flows through the Huron National Forest and was once used to float logs to the sawmills in East Tawas and Oscoda; now, of course, it's more popular with paddlers.

The national forest is favored by a wide range of outdoor enthusiasts, including morel hunters who visit in the spring, backpackers, swimmers, and cross-country skiers. Trout fishing is a good bet in most lakes and streams, as well as in the legendary Au Sable River.

The forest's famous **River Road Scenic Byway** runs 22 miles along the southern bank of the Au Sable. The byway passes some of the most spectacular scenery in the eastern Lower Peninsula, and provides stunning vistas of tree-banked reservoirs and views of wildlife that include everything from bald eagles to spawning salmon. Along the way, you'll also pass the **Lumberman's Monument,** a 9-foot bronze statue that depicts the area's early loggers and overlooks the river valley 10 miles northwest of East Tawas. A visitors center here houses

- Pack up all trash and store it on board until you can dispose of it properly at your trip's end.
- Leave all historical resources, plants, birds, and marine creatures as you find them.
- Respect all wildlife; do not approach, harass, or feed any animals that you see.
- Be considerate of anglers and other paddlers, avoid crossing fishing lines, and stay to the right of motorboats.
- If you're taking an overnight paddling trip and plan to camp somewhere, be sure to camp on durable surfaces away from the water, and minimize the impact from campfires (if they're even allowed where you're staying).

Besides the items already mentioned, you should bring the following essentials with you:

- anchor (if you plan to snorkel or camp) and some rope
- area maps and NOAA nautical charts
- bilge pump and sponge
- binoculars
- camera and extra batteries
- compass or GPS
- duct tape
- extra waterproof bags
- first-aid kit
- insect repellent
- lip balm with SPF
- long-sleeved shirt for extra protection
- pocketknife or multipurpose tool
- repair kit
- signaling devices such as a flashlight, flare, mirror, or air horn
- sunglasses
- sunscreen
- 360-degree light for operating your vessel at night
- towels, extra clothing, and extra shoes in a waterproof bag
- VHF or weather radio to monitor weather forecasts
- wide-brimmed hat

For more information about canoeing and kayaking in Michigan, including paddling destinations and liveries, consult the **Michigan Department of Natural Resources** (DNR, Parks and Recreation Division, 517/284-7275, www.michigan.gov/dnr) and the **Michigan Association of Paddlesport Providers** (MAPP, www.michigancanoe.com), or visit www.canoeingmichiganrivers.com.

NORTHEAST MICHIGAN

interpretive displays that explore the logging legacy. Just a short walk away, a cliff plummets in a near-vertical 160-foot drop to the Au Sable River below. It offers jaw-dropping views of the valley and marks the beginning of the **Stairway to Discovery,** an unusual interpretive nature trail that descends 260 steps to the river and earns distinction as the nation's only nature trail located entirely on a staircase.

Also in the national forest, the **Tuttle Marsh Wildlife Management Area,** about seven miles west of Au Sable, was created in the spring of 1990 as a cooperative effort by the U.S. Forest Service, the state's Department of Natural Resources, and Ducks Unlimited. Once an area filled with sad-looking shrubs and scattered patches of grass, the wetlands now attract a significant number of migrating waterfowl, shorebirds, and sandhill cranes, as well as muskrats, minks, beavers, and bald eagles.

Backpackers looking for a wilderness camping experience should try the **Hoist Lakes Trail System.** Backcountry camping is allowed just about anywhere in this large, rugged area of more than 10,000 acres. Nearly 20 miles of trails (hiking only) wander through secondgrowth forest over gently rolling wooded terrain, around marshes, past beaver floodings,

THE TINY BIRD WITH THE HUGE FOLLOWING

To call **Kirtland's warbler** endangered is an understatement – save for parts of Wisconsin and Canada, several counties in Michigan's Upper and northern Lower Peninsulas, especially the region around the Au Sable River between Grayling and Mio, are the only places in the world where the bird is known to breed today. The world population is estimated at less than 1,400 pairs.

A tiny blue-gray songbird with a yellow breast, Kirtland's warbler winters in the Bahamas, then returns to the Au Sable River area, where it subsists on insects and blueberries and searches for the proper habitat to suit its picky nesting requirements: young stands of jack pine with small grassy clearings. It builds nests on the low-lying branches of jack pines between 5 and 20 feet high; when the trees get much higher, the warbler seeks out younger trees.

The bird's precarious plight is a classic case of habitat loss. When forest fires occur naturally, jack pines are one of the first trees to regenerate in burned areas. But decades of logging and fire suppression led to fewer forest fires, which in turn led to fewer young jack pines. To help the warbler, the U.S. Forest Service, the U.S. Fish and Wildlife Service, the Michigan Department of Natural Resources, and other government agencies now do nature's job, cultivating, harvesting, and replanting acres of jack pines in the **Kirtland's Warbler Wildlife Management Area, in** order to keep an ample supply of young trees suitable for the warbler's nesting needs. Environmentalists also assist the warbler by controlling the region's population of brown-headed cowbirds, which routinely take over warbler nests and outcompete their nest-mates for food.

Not surprisingly, the bird's breeding grounds are off-limits to the public during the May-August nesting season. From mid-May through late June, however, guided, three-hour tours (7am daily, $10 pp) are led by the U.S. Forest Service, beginning at the Mio Ranger Station, and from mid-May through early July, the U.S. Fish and Wildlife Service and Michigan Audubon Society jointly offer guided tours (7am Mon.-Fri., 7am and 11am Sat.-Sun. and holidays, free) of the same area, usually departing from the Ramada Inn in Grayling. Of course, actual sightings aren't guaranteed. For more information about the tours, contact the **Forest Service's Mio Ranger Station** (989/826-3252) or **Seney National Wildlife Refuge** (906/586-9851).

and across streams. The forest teems with deer, bears, coyotes, foxes, owls, hawks, and songbirds, along with turkeys, woodcocks, grouse, and other game birds. Fishing includes good numbers of bass and panfish. The 6.1-mile **Reid Lake Foot Travel Area** marks another great hiking area surrounded by some of the forest's most imposing hardwoods.

About 10 miles west of East Tawas, the **Corsair Trail System** bills itself as "Michigan's Cross-Country Ski Capital," but it is equally popular with hikers and backpackers. Also part of the Huron National Forest, the well-marked trail system (groomed in winter) includes more than 15 loops totaling 44 miles. One writer described this sprawling complex as

"a web spun by a spider high on LSD." Choose-your-own adventures range from a short jaunt along Silver Creek to a two-day trek through the entire system.

Full of rolling hills, deep glacial potholes, and a beautiful hardwood forest, the **Island Lake Recreation Area** offers a quiet and beautiful alternative to the more heavily used recreation areas. You'll find it seven miles north of Rose City via M-33 and CR-486. Out of the way and relatively small, it hides a swimming beach, a 17-site campground, and a 65-acre lake that supports perch, bluegills, and large- and smallmouth bass. A self-guiding nature trail explains the area's natural history and notes points of interest along the way.

◖ HOUGHTON AND HIGGINS LAKES

Near the southern end of Northeast Michigan, in Roscommon County, lie two of the state's largest inland lakes—22,000-acre Houghton Lake and 10,200-acre Higgins Lake—both of which entice plenty of anglers, boaters, canoeists, swimmers, hikers, and campers during the summer months. In winter, this area is also popular among hunters, ice fishers, and cross-country skiers.

Beaches

Both lakes present a number of terrific beaches. On Higgins Lake, you'll find the **North Higgins Lake State Park Day Use Area,** situated on North Higgins Lake Drive, and the **South Higgins Lake State Park Day Use Area,** located on CR-100. Each offers a sandy swimming beach, a bathhouse, a playground, picnic shelters, and a boat launch. You'll need an annual Recreation Passport ($11 residents/$30.50 nonresidents) or a day-use pass ($8.40) in order to utilize either of these beaches.

Meanwhile, on Houghton Lake, you'll discover the **Roscommon Township Beach** (Sanford St.), which has a pleasant sandy beach on the south shore, ideal for swimmers of all ages. The area also offers a sheltered picnic area, a small playground, and restrooms.

Boating and Fishing

Houghton and Higgins Lakes are both well known among boaters, canoeists, and anglers. Together, the two enormous lakes offer a dozen launch sites and tons of water to explore. Although Houghton and Higgins are particularly ideal for those with their own canoes, kayaks, and fishing boats, several facilities do rent boats as well. For more information about renting pontoon and fishing boats, check out **Houghton Lake Marina** (13710 W. Shore Dr., 989/422-7257). It's a terrific way for those without boats of their own to enjoy drifting around the lake, savoring the sunshine, or trying their luck at snagging bass, bluegill, walleye, and pike.

Accommodations and Food

You'll find a decent variety of lodgings in the area, including chain hotels. The **Comfort Inn** (200 Cloverleaf Ln., Houghton Lake, 989/422-7829, www.comfortinn.com, $63-149 d) and the **Comfort Suites Lakeside** (100 Clearview Dr., Houghton Lake, 989/422-4000, www.comfortsuiteslakeside.com, $139-350 d) each offer terrific access to the lakes as well as numerous water-related amenities, such as canoeing packages and watercraft rentals. Comfort Suites also features a 9,000-square-foot water park, a boat dock, and the Blue Bayou Restaurant and Lounge, with a deck bar that overlooks the majestic lake.

Houghton and Higgins Lakes both have numerous campgrounds, too, some catering to RVs, others allowing both tent and RV camping. On Houghton Lake, you'll find the **Houghton Lake Travel Park Campground** (370 Cloverleaf Ln., Houghton Lake, 989/422-3931, www.houghtonlaketravelparkcampground.com, Apr.-Oct., $30-43 daily), which has something for everyone. On Higgins Lake, check out the **Higgins Lake KOA** (3800 W. Federal Hwy., Roscommon, 989/275-8151, www.koa.com, $28-34 daily).

After a long day of boating, fishing, swimming, or exploring the area, satisfy your hunger at the nearby **Buccilli's Pizza** (2949 W. Houghton Lake Dr., Houghton Lake, 989/366-5374, www.buccillispizza.com, 11am 10pm daily, $5-19), which offers tasty pizza for dine-in, takeout, or delivery.

Information and Services

For more information about Houghton and Higgins Lakes, contact the **Houghton Lake Area Tourism & Convention Bureau** (9091 W. Lake City Rd., Houghton Lake, 989/422-2002 or 800/676-5330, www.visithoughton-lake.com). If you require other services, such as banks and groceries, your best bet would probably be to drive north on I-75 to Grayling or Gaylord.

Getting There and Around

The easiest way to reach the lakes is via car.

NORTHEAST MICHIGAN

From West Branch, for instance, you can simply take M-55 West, merge onto I-75 North/M-55 West, and continue onto M-55 West, which hugs the southern shore of Houghton Lake; the 28-mile trip from West Branch to the town of Houghton Lake usually takes about a half hour. From Grayling, meanwhile, you can reach North Higgins Lake State Park by heading south on I-75, continuing onto US-127 South, and turning left onto North Higgins Lake Drive, a 13-mile trip that usually takes about 16 minutes. Once you reach the lakes, you can explore the area via boat, bike, or foot.

Grayling Area

From Bay City, I-75 cuts across the northeastern part of the state until it bisects the North Country near Grayling. Several clean, clear, and immensely popular rivers—most notably, the Au Sable and the Manistee—corkscrew their way through the region, making Grayling the hub of one of the Lower Peninsula's leading recreational areas.

First classified in 1884, the grayling once was the only game fish to inhabit the upper Au Sable system. Related to trout and salmon and characterized by a long, wavy dorsal fin, grayling were considered both a fine sporting fish and a delicious eating fish—a fatal combination. The thrill of landing one drew the attention of sportfishers near and far, who came by railroad to Grayling, soon a bustling center of fishing trips. With no regulations at the time, anglers snatched grayling from area rivers by the thousands. The wanton fishing, combined with the declining water quality caused by riverbank erosion from logging, put a quick end to the species. Grayling were rare in Grayling by 1900 and extinct by 1930.

Alas, the town's namesake fish may be gone, but we've learned a few lessons about protecting species and their habitat along the way. Today, Grayling offers some of the finest trout fishing in the Midwest—even the nation—and is a key destination for anglers, canoeists, hunters, hikers, mountain bikers, cross-country skiing enthusiasts, and snowmobilers.

RECREATION
Hiking and Biking
Popular with equestrians, hikers, cross-country skiers, and snowshoers, the 220-mile **Michigan Shore-to-Shore Riding and Hiking Trail** traverses the entire Lower Peninsula. In this area, it skirts the north end of the George Mason River Retreat Area, passing through pine plantations, stands of hardwood, and along the gentle Au Sable. Other good area access points include the McKinley Trail Camp in Oscoda and across from the Curtisville Store in Glennie.

The rolling terrain of Crawford County makes for some great mountain biking, and even better, the local tourism council actually encourages it—a rare thing in the Midwest. The Grayling Visitors Bureau recommends the following near Grayling: **Michigan Cross Country Cycle Trail,** a great technical singletrack that "goes for miles and miles." Access it where it crosses Military Road, 0.5 mile north of the North Higgins Lake State Park exit off US-27. Also check out the **Hanson Hills Recreation Area** (7601 Old Lake Rd., Grayling, 989/348-9266, www.hansonhills.org, $2 donation suggested), which offers challenging terrain that includes some sandy stretches, and **Wakely Lake,** situated 10 miles east of Grayling via M-72 and featuring three loops of 4.5, 5, and 7 miles. To secure a required parking pass for the Wakely Lake area, contact the **Mio Ranger District** (107 McKinley Rd., Mio, 989/826-3252, www.fs.usda.gov, 8am-4:30pm Mon.-Fri.) of the Huron National Forest.

Canoeing
Scenic streams crisscross the forests around

Grayling. The Boardman, Manistee, Pine, Rifle, and Au Sable Rivers meander through wetlands, across dunes, and past tree-covered hills. Canoeing ranks among the area's most popular pastimes, with a number of liveries offering adventures on the Au Sable and other area rivers. Even novice paddlers can handle the easygoing currents of these waterways as they scan the shoreline for deer, beavers, black bears, and winsome river otters. The area's canoe liveries are concentrated in Grayling.

Flowing east out of Grayling, the Au Sable coils through the **Au Sable State Forest.** Designated a state natural river with stretches of the main stream protected as a national wild and scenic river, the Au Sable flows past wooded islands and stretches of white sand. At night, weary paddlers can bed down at one of several state and national forest campgrounds along the river's shore. For day-trippers, the most popular take-outs are at Stephan Landing (about a 4-hour leisurely paddle from Grayling) and Wakely Landing, a 5.5-hour trip at a similar pace.

Recognized for its excellent trout fishing and often overlooked by paddlers is the Au Sable's South Branch, in which you can also launch a boat. You'll find landings at Chase Bridge on the south end and at Smith Bridge, 11 miles to the north.

The Au Sable can be a victim of its own success, though, with raucous crowds sometimes floating the river en masse on hot summer weekends. If you're looking for a party, this is the place, but be aware that local authorities watch for intoxication carefully and fine liberally. (Glass containers, kegs, and Styrofoam coolers are prohibited on the Au Sable to keep down the partying and the littering.) If you're looking for a more peaceful experience, avoid the party set by departing during the week or arranging to paddle a stretch farther outside Grayling, if you can talk an outfitter into it. Alternatively, many paddlers find the Manistee River less of a scene. For a complete list of liveries in the Grayling region, contact the **Grayling Visitors Bureau** (213 N. James St., 800/937-8837, www.grayling-mi.com).

As a testament to its paddling popularity, Grayling is the site of one of the country's few canoeing festivals, the **AuSable River Canoe Marathon** (www.ausablecanoemarathon.org). Held in late July, the 120-mile route runs from Grayling to Oscoda on Lake Huron and ranks as North America's longest and most difficult nonstop canoe race. An estimated 30,000 fans turn out, many following the world-class athletes in the grueling race down the river, which requires some 55,000 paddle strokes and more than 14 hours to complete. It's worth going just to watch the thrilling 9am shotgun start, when more than 50 teams carrying canoes on their heads race through downtown Grayling to the launch site.

Fishing

Fly-fishing enthusiasts from all over the country make the pilgrimage to the Au Sable, where the combination of spring-fed waters, clean gravel river bottoms, and all the right insect hatches make for stellar trout fishing. All along the area's rivers, you'll spot anglers plying their sport, standing midstream in hip waders, unfurling a long arc of lemon-colored line across the river with their fly rods, or casting from a flat-bottom Au Sable riverboat specifically designed for drifting these shallow waters. Many congregate just east of town in a 10-mile catch-and-release area known as "the holy waters."

While the Grayling Visitors Bureau will help you link up with fishing guides, you also can try your luck from shore. (Obtain a license—available at local shops and gas stations—and check fishing regulations first.) Both the Manistee and Au Sable pass through several miles of state and federal lands, so you won't have much trouble finding public access.

Farther southeast, the Rifle River and its upper tributaries have earned reputations for yielding good catches of brown, rainbow, and brook trout. Some steelhead and chinook salmon are caught on the river's upper reaches, and pike, bass, and panfish are pulled from the dozen or so lakes and ponds in Rifle River Recreation Area, many of which have public access sites.

NORTHEAST MICHIGAN

REBUILDING AMERICA:
THE CIVILIAN CONSERVATION CORPS

By 1933, the United States was cracked deeply by the Great Depression. One after another, factories and businesses shut down. Lines at soup kitchens straggled around city blocks. Nearly 14 million Americans were unemployed.

Along with an economy in ruin, President Franklin D. Roosevelt saw an environment in ruin as well. While virgin forests had once covered 800 million acres of the United States, old growth had dwindled to just 100 million acres. Erosion had ruined more than 100 million acres of the nation's tillable land, and more was eroding at an alarming rate.

In March 1933, President Roosevelt asked Congress for the power to create the Civilian Conservation Corps (CCC). A New Deal program, the proposed corps would recruit 250,000 unemployed, unmarried young men to work on federal- and state-owned land for "the prevention of forest fires, floods, and soil erosion, plant, pest and disease control."

As proposed, the Labor Department would recruit the young men, while the War Department would run the program, housing, clothing, and feeding the men in work camps, and paying them a monthly stipend of $30–$25 of which had to be sent home to their families. The Department of Agriculture and Interior planned the work projects, which included reforesting cutover land, preventing forest fires, developing state parks, and building dams, bridges, and roads. Along with the field work, education was a hallmark of the CCC. Camps helped members obtain their high school diplomas, and provided supplemental training in at least 30 different vocations.

The program was not without controversy. Some criticized the cost; others balked at the idea of military control over labor, comparing it to fascism and Hitlerism. Still others contended young men should be with their families, or, as Michigan congressman Fred Crawford suggested, at work in farm fields rather than in "some camp in the woods to participate in a face-lifting operation on Mother Earth."

But Roosevelt saw it differently. Through the CCC, he believed two invaluable and impoverished resources – the nation's young men

ACCOMMODATIONS AND FOOD

For paddlers, you can't do better than ◖ **Penrod's Au Sable River Resort** (100 Maple St., 888/467-4837, www.penrodscanoe.com, $60-96 d), where cute cabins line a peaceful bend in the river. Penrod's adjacent paddle-sport center rents canoes, kayaks, and mountain bikes, and offers shuttle service for river trips. If you care more about location than amenities and are coming to fish, **Gates Au Sable Lodge** (471 Stephan Bridge Rd., 989/348-8462, www.gateslodge.com, $90 d) has motel-style rooms with a perfect setting right on the banks of the Au Sable. Also right on the Au Sable, **Borchers Au Sable Canoe Livery with Bed & Breakfast** (101 Maple St., 989/348-4921, www.canoeborchers.com, $78-98 d) invites you to slow to the pace of the river on its wraparound porch.

Hungry hunters, paddlers, and bird-watchers head to **Spikes Keg O Nails** (301 N. James St., 989/348-7113, www.spikes-grayling.com, 10am-1:30am Mon.-Sat., noon-1:30am Sun., $6-19) for a burger. Try the "World Famous Spikeburger," topped with everything.

Camping

You'll find plenty of good, inexpensive public campgrounds in the Grayling area. **Hartwick Pines State Park** (4216 Ranger Rd., 989/348-7068, annual $11 Recreation Passport for Michigan residents or $8.40 day-use fee/$30.50 yearly Recreation Passport for nonresidents required) in Grayling offers clean, modern sites ($16-33 daily) that fill up fast. You might find and its land – could be brought together in an attempt to save both. In his message to Congress, Roosevelt declared that "we face a future of soil erosion and timber famine" and that the CCC would "conserve our precious national resources" and "pay dividends to the present and future generations."

The measure was easily passed, and so was Roosevelt's goal of 250,000 workers. On April 17, 1933, the nation's first CCC camp opened in the George Washington National Forest in Virginia. By July 1, 250,000 men were at work in more than 1,460 camps –t he fastest large-scale mobilization of men (including World War I) in U.S. history. By 1935, "Roosevelt's Tree Army" had ballooned to more than 500,000 workers.

Evidence of the CCC's work remains apparent throughout the Great Lakes region. CCC workers eradicated white pine blister rust in Minnesota, built fire towers and fire roads in Wisconsin, and improved hundreds of miles of fishing streams in Michigan. They built park shelters in Ohio, campgrounds in Indiana, and trails in Illinois. They planted thousands of acres of trees, fought countless wildfires, and built hundreds of bridges and buildings. They even moved moose from Isle Royale to the Upper Peninsula for wildlife studies.

By 1936, the CCC was above reproach, supported by more than 80 percent of Americans and even endorsed by Roosevelt's political opponents. With the bombing of Pearl Harbor in 1941, however, the nation soon had a more pressing duty for its young men. The nation's entry into World War II, along with an improving economy, meant the end of the CCC by 1942. But its legacy, like the trees it planted, continues to grow in our nation's parks and forests.

The **Civilian Conservation Corps Museum** (11747 N. Higgins Lake Dr., Roscommon, 989/348-6178, www.michigan.gov/ccc-museum, 10am-4pm daily Memorial Day-Labor Day, free) uses various photographs, artifacts, and outdoor exhibits to tell the story of Michigan's CCC crews. Situated in North Higgins Lake State Park, the CCC Museum celebrates the efforts of more than 100,000 young men who strived to improve Michigan's forests during the Great Depression. Just note that, although the museum itself is free to visit, you'll need to pay a day-use fee or show your annual Recreation Passport to enter the state park.

---

a little more solitude (and fewer RVs) at the **Au Sable State Forest** (5.5 miles east of Grayling via N. Down River Rd., 989/826-3211, annual $11 Recreation Passport for Michigan residents or $8.40 day-use fee/$30.50 yearly Recreation Passport for nonresidents required), which offers several rustic campgrounds ($13 daily).

INFORMATION AND SERVICES

For more information, contact the **Grayling Visitors Bureau** (213 N. James St., 800/937-8837, www.grayling-mi.com). Grayling has a limited number of services; if necessary, you can always head north to Gaylord to stock up on supplies prior to an outing in the great outdoors. If an emergency occurs, dial **911** from any cell or public phone.

GETTING THERE AND AROUND

While **Greyhound** (989/348-8682 or 800/231-2222, www.greyhound.com) and **Indian Trails** (800/292-3831, www.indiantrails.com) both provide bus service to Grayling (500 Norway St.), most visitors arrive via car, truck, motorcycle, or RV. Given that the town sits at the junction of I-75 and M-72—and not far north from where I-75 and US-127 converge—it's easy to reach whether you're headed from Detroit to the southeast, Mackinaw City to the north, Traverse City to the west, or Chicago to the southwest. From downtown Detroit, for instance, you can simply take I-375 North, I-75 North, and the I-75 Business Route to reach Grayling; without traffic, the 205-mile trip requires less than three hours. From Mackinaw

City, you can access Grayling via I-75 South, an 85-mile trip that usually takes about 80 minutes, while from Traverse City, you can typically reach Grayling, which lies 51 miles away, in about an hour via M-72 East. If, on the other hand, you're venturing here from Chicago, just follow I-90 East and I-94 East through Illinois and Indiana, cross the Michigan state line, continue onto I-196 North/US-31 North and I-196 East, merge onto US-131 North toward Cadillac, and take M-72 East to Grayling. Just be advised that, en route from the Windy City, parts of I-90 East and I-94 East serve as the Indiana Toll Road. No matter how you reach Grayling, though, you can easily get around by car, bike, and, to a certain extent, foot.

GEORGE MASON RIVER RETREAT AREA

George Mason, an area industrialist, so loved this area that he bequeathed 1,500 acres to the state for its preservation in 1954. Located about 15 miles east of Grayling on Canoe Harbor Road, the George Mason River Retreat Area is considered part of the Au Sable State Forest. Subsequent land acquisitions have nearly tripled the size of this natural area, which provides ample opportunity to fish, canoe, or hike for free along a stretch of the South Branch of the Au Sable River. For more information about the George Mason River Retreat Area, which is open year-round, contact the **Roscommon Field Office** (989/275-4622) of the Michigan Department of Natural Resources (www.michigan.gov/dnr).

◖ HARTWICK PINES STATE PARK

The majestic white pine may be the state tree, but few virgin stands remain today. One of the last can be seen at the **Hartwick Pines State Park** (4216 Ranger Rd., 989/348-7068, annual $11 Recreation Passport for Michigan residents or $8.40 day-use fee/$30.50 yearly Recreation Passport for nonresidents required), one of the largest parks in the state. A century ago, more than 13 million of the state's 38 million acres were covered with the majestic trees, but by the

early 1900s more than 160 billion board feet of timber had been harvested. By the 1920s, these once majestic forests were denuded wastelands.

More than 250,000 visitors stroll through the pines annually, marveling at trees that have been here since before the Revolutionary War. Long a popular stop for vacationers heading north, the state park has been improved over the years, with a superb visitors center, a walkway to the pines that's accessible to both wheelchairs and strollers, and a steam sawmill that's part of an extensive logging museum area. The park is also the site of the **Hartwick Pines State Forest Festivals:** four different events held throughout the summer, including **Sawdust Days, Wood Shaving Days, Black Iron Days,** and **Old Time Days.**

The park's **Michigan Forest Visitors Center** boasts a 100-seat auditorium; a 14-minute audiovisual show on "The Forest: Michigan's Renewable Resource," which is presented every 30 minutes; and an exhibit hall that concentrates on forest management. Ironically, many of the displays were funded by forestry products companies, so don't expect to see explorations of the negative environmental effects of logging.

The 49-acre virgin tract of white and red pines is the main attraction. Reaching as high as 10 stories, the majestic trees were slated for cutting in the mid 1890s. Fortunately for us, the logging company charged with felling the trees was forced to suspend operations due to economic problems. In 1927, the trees and the surrounding 8,000 acres were purchased from the lumber company and donated to the state for a park.

The self-guided **Old Growth Forest Trail** connects the pines with the visitors center, a 1.25-mile blacktopped path that weaves among the regal giants, including the Monarch. Once the tract's largest specimen at 155 feet, a windstorm destroyed the top 40 feet of the now-diseased and dying tree. Part of nature's cycle, several other immense white pines tower nearby, ready to take its place in the record books.

The pines and museums overshadow the rest

of the park, but don't overlook it yourself. With more than 9,600 acres, it offers plenty to do besides admire tall trees. Signs and other displays mark the eight-mile **Scenic Drive,** about two miles north of the main entrance, encouraging visitors to explore the woods and natural world around them. Hiking and biking trails include 17 miles of easy trails open to mountain bikes in summer and cross-country skiers in winter. The Au Sable River Trail (no bikes) is one of the loveliest. It crosses the East Branch of the legendary river and passes a rare forest of virgin hemlock, saved from the saw by a sudden drop in the price of its bark, which was once used for tanning leather. The two-mile Mertz Grade Nature Trail loops through the park and past an old logging railroad grade before linking up with the Virgin Pines Trail behind the visitors center.

Open year-round, the park is especially popular in the spring, when wildflowers bloom, and in the early fall, when the colorful hardwoods explode in a riot of fiery reds, yellows, and oranges.

Gaylord Area

North of Grayling on I-75, Gaylord was officially organized in 1875 as "Otsego," an Indian word that means "beautiful lake." Located at the north end of long, skinny Otsego Lake, Gaylord remains a basically rural village with a year-round population of roughly 3,600. But its topography lures vacationers by the thousands.

Gaylord sits on the highest point in southern Michigan, which inspired the town to morph itself into "the Alpine Village." Its Main Street is decorated with balconies, blossoming window boxes, even a glockenspiel on the Glen's Market grocery store. And while more Polish and German descendants reside here than Swiss, the townspeople happily don dirndls and lederhosen each July during the annual Alpenfest. Some visitors come for the culture, but Gaylord offers plenty of outdoor attractions as well—from world-class golf to accessible lakes to bugling elk.

SIGHTS
Call of the Wild Museum
While this unassuming museum has been around for decades (during which the displays haven't changed all that much), the **Call of the Wild Museum** (850 S. Wisconsin Ave., 989/732-4336, www.gocallofthewild.com, 9am-9pm daily June 15-Labor Day, 9:30am-6pm Mon.-Sat. Sept.-mid-June, $7 adults, $4.50 children 5-13) is still a terrific place to take your children for a little while. Many of its wildlife displays come packed with audio features, bringing the animals to life. Creepy, yet fascinating, the two projected images of Joseph Bailly help to educate visitors about what life was like in the early 1800s, when he (one of the area's first trappers) initially ventured into the Michigan area.

Otsego Lake State Park
Established in 1920, **Otsego Lake State Park** (7136 Old 27 S, 989/732-5485) is a boating enthusiast's dream. The lake itself is long and wide, allowing ample room for boats and all manner of other water sports. This park has been a popular, family-friendly destination for nine decades.

ALPENFEST
You can't miss the distinctive architecture that's earned Gaylord its "Alpine Village" moniker. To celebrate the community's Alpine heritage, part of Main Street is blocked off every July for the annual **Alpenfest** (989/732-6333, www.gaylordalpenfest.com). Established in the mid-1960s, the five-day event features traditional dancing, costumed musicians, yodeling and pie-eating contests, an "Edelweiss" sing-along, and plenty of ethnic food, from sauerkraut to strudel to pasties, in addition to carnival favorites like hot dogs, ice cream, and, yes, beer.

NORTHEAST MICHIGAN

MICHIGAN'S ELK

© GAYLORD AREA CTB

Once a common sight in the Lower Peninsula, the eastern elk disappeared from Michigan in the late 1870s. Biologists made several attempts to reintroduce the animal to the state throughout the early 1900s, but it wasn't until the successful release of seven Rocky Mountain elk in 1918 that the mammals once again were seen regularly in northeastern Michigan.

Wildlife biologists today believe that the region's elk are descendants of those early animals. They roam a 600-square-mile area primarily east and north of Gaylord in Otsego, Cheboygan, Presque Isle, and Montmorency Counties. The heaviest concentration is north of Gaylord in the 95,000-acre **Pigeon River**

Country State Forest (9966 Twin Lakes Rd., Vanderbilt, 989/983-4101).

The best way to plan a visit is to stop by the Pigeon River forestry field office off Sturgeon Valley Road. To reach the office from Vanderbilt, drive east on Sturgeon Valley Road about 13 miles (past a prime elk-viewing site), turn left onto Hardwood Lake Road, and continue for about one mile to the office. Although the office hours vary seasonally, the staff, when present, will provide helpful maps and suggest ideal areas and times to view the elk. That said, fall rutting season often proves to be the most spectacular, when the bulls throw their heads back and fill the forests with eerie bugling sounds, their distinctive mating call.

the Call of the Wild Museum

The open-air "Alpenstrasse," an arts-and-crafts village showcases the wares of more than 60 Michigan artists and artisans. The town even makes room for several amusement park rides and carnival games.

SPORTS AND RECREATION

Golf

But Gaylord is best known for its golf, boasting the largest number of courses in the state: more than 20, with more on the drawing board all the time. The area around Gaylord, in fact, has emerged as America's premier golf mecca, with the thickest concentration of designer courses anywhere in the United States, including those by well-known designers such as Robert Trent Jones Sr., Tom Fazio, and Al Watrous.

If you have the time, consider visiting at least three of the area's favored golf clubs. Head first to Onaway, on M-68, where you'll find the **Black Lake Golf Club** (2800 Maxon Rd., 989/733-4653, www.blacklakegolf.com, daily Apr.-Oct., $55-70 pp). Operated by the UAW, this magnificent golf course is part of the union's 1,000-acre family center, which sits astride picturesque Black Lake.

Another winning choice is **Garland Lodge & Resort** (4700 N. Red Oak Rd., Lewiston, 989/786-2211 or 877/442-7526, www.garlandusa.com, daily May-Oct., $75-120 pp). Considered one of the state's most beautiful resorts, this longstanding option presents four magnificent golf courses amid the woods of northeastern Michigan.

Lastly, schedule a tee time at the lovely **Treetops Resort** (3962 Wilkinson Rd., Gaylord, 989/732-6711 or 888/873-3867, www.treetops.com, daily Apr.-Oct., $45-135 pp). This year-round resort keeps visitors busy with downhill skiing in winter, activities like tennis and biking in summer, and, of course, five stunning golf courses.

Hiking

The Shingle Mill Pathway links up with the **High Country Pathway,** an 80-mile route that snakes east through state land in four counties, passing through a wilderness of rolling hills and

an Alpenfest crowd

several creeks feeding the Black River. A side trail leads to Shoepac Lake and the Sinkholes Pathway, where the land is pitted with dry sinkholes and sinkhole lakes, formed when underground limestone caves collapsed.

Elk may be the main attraction at the Pigeon River Country State Forest, but beavers bring visitors to the **Big Bear Lake Nature Pathway,** 17 miles east of Gaylord. Part of the Mackinaw State Forest trail system, the pathway's two loops total just over 2 miles and lead through a variety of landscape and habitats home to deer, porcupines, woodcocks, waterfowl, and beavers. The shorter, 0.8-mile Beaver Lodge Loop circles a pond with an active beaver colony. The longer Eagles Roost Trail carves a wide, 2-mile loop that threads its way through upland hardwoods and through a dense stand of aspen and an open area carpeted with wildflowers in the summer. Both trails begin and end at the **Big Bear Lake State Forest Campground** (989/732-3541, $15 daily), on the north shore of Big Bear Lake, accessible via Bear Lake Road.

Snowmobiling

Gaylord is the crossroads of many snowmobiling trails (www.visitgaylord.com/snowmobile). With over 150 inches of average snowfall a year, Gaylord is a snowmobiler's dream. Many of the state's best trails either start or pass through the area. If you're looking for a great ride, the **Gaylord-Frederic-Grayling-Blue Bear Loop** will give you a two- to four-day adventure.

ACCOMMODATIONS AND FOOD

The Gaylord area is best known for its golf resorts, and they can offer some good package deals, especially for families. **◖ Garland Lodge & Resort** (4700 N. Red Oak Rd., Lewiston, 989/786-2211, www.garlandusa.com, $99-499 d) has a lot of stay-and-play deals where golf is included in the price. If you're just looking for a simple motel room, you'll find several of the usual chains—Super 8, Days Inn, Comfort Inn, etc.—near I-75.

The same Greek American family has

© LAURA MARTONE

the Garland Lodge & Resort

been running the **Sugar Bowl** (216 W. Main St., 989/732-5524, 7am-11pm daily, $6-22) since 1919. Specialties include Lake Superior whitefish, scampi, Athenian chicken, and other favorite ethnic dishes, all prepared on an open hearth. Tip: They serve morel mushroom dishes in season, usually May. Don't miss the vintage photos of historic Gaylord on the walls.

Gobbler's Famous Turkey Dinners (900 S. Otsego, 989/732-9005, 10am-9pm daily, $5-14) prepares more than 80,000 pounds of bird annually, all from scratch and served with mashed potatoes, biscuits, gravy, and dressing. The portion sizes are legendary. There's also hand-breaded fresh fish and barbecued ribs if you don't do turkey.

Between Gaylord and Lewiston is the single-traffic-light town of Johannesburg, where you'll find 🄲 **Paul's Pub** (10757 E. M-32, 989/732-5005, www.paulspubandcatering.com, 10am-midnight Mon.-Thurs., 10am-2am Fri.-Sat., 8am-midnight Sun., $6-28), with its wide assortment of beers and the best fried

perch in Michigan. They also have quite the Sunday brunch, but get here early. This local favorite can get pretty busy on the weekends.

Camping
Pigeon River Country State Forest (off Sturgeon Valley Rd., 989/983-4101, $15 daily) offers 29 rustic sites in a nice secluded setting. For waterfront sites, try **Otsego Lake State Park** (7136 Old 27 S, 989/732-5485, annual $11 Recreation Passport for Michigan residents or $8.40 day-use fee/$30.50 yearly Recreation Passport for nonresidents required), with 206 sites ($16-26 daily) on or near Otsego Lake.

INFORMATION AND SERVICES
For more information about the Gaylord area, contact the **Gaylord Area Convention & Tourism Bureau** (101 W. Main St., 989/732-4000, www.gaylordmichigan.net). For local news, consult the *Gaylord Herald Times* (www.gaylordheraldtimes.com).

Despite its relatively small size, Gaylord offers a wide range of services, including a post office, several banks and gas stations, and numerous stores, from Wal-Mart to Home Depot to Glen's Market. If a medical emergency occurs during your visit, dial **911** or consult **Otsego Memorial Hospital** (825 N. Center Ave., 989/731-2100, www.myomh.org).

GETTING THERE AND AROUND
While **Greyhound** (989/732-9063 or 800/231-2222, www.greyhound.com) and **Indian Trails** (800/292-3831, www.indiantrails.com) both provide bus service to Gaylord (1041 W. Main St.), most visitors arrive via car, truck, motorcycle, or RV. After all, given that the town sits at the junction of I-75 and M-32, it's an easy place to reach whether you're coming from Detroit, Sault Ste. Marie, Traverse City, or Chicago. From downtown Detroit, for instance, you can simply follow I-375 North and I-75 North to reach Gaylord; without traffic, the 232-mile

© DANIEL MARTONE

Paul's Pub in Johannesburg

trip takes about 3.25 hours. From Sault Ste. Marie, you can access Gaylord via I-75 South, which crosses the Mackinac Bridge (a toll bridge) before continuing south to Gaylord, a 116-mile trip that usually takes less than 2 hours, while from Traverse City, you can simply take M-72 East, US-131 North, CR-42, and M-32 East to reach Gaylord, a 62-mile trip that typically takes about 80 minutes.

If, on the other hand, you're venturing here from Chicago, just follow I-90 East and I-94 East through Illinois and Indiana, cross the Michigan state line, continue onto I-196 North/US-31 North and I-196 East, merge onto US-131 North toward Cadillac, and take CR-42 and M-32 East to Gaylord. Just be advised that, en route from the Windy City, parts of I-90 East and I-94 East serve as the Indiana Toll Road. Note that, no matter how you reach Gaylord, you can easily get around by car, bike, and, to a certain extent, foot.

PIGEON RIVER COUNTRY STATE FOREST

With a shaggy chocolate mane and a crown of showy antlers, the eastern elk may be Michigan's most spectacular mammal, sometimes weighing in at close to 1,000 pounds. Elk are rare in the Midwest, but about 1,000 of them—the largest free-roaming elk herd east of the Mississippi River—populate this state forest and the surrounding countryside.

Although its primary draw is the opportunity to spot the elk herd, this 97,000-acre state forest north of Gaylord has miles of hiking trails, good fishing, and scenic rustic campgrounds. The **Shingle Mill Pathway** passes through deep woods and across rolling, hilly terrain. Keep an eye out for the forest's "other" wildlife, which includes bears, coyotes, bobcats, beavers, otters, woodcocks, turkeys, bald eagles, ospreys, loons, and blue herons. For more information on the state forest, stop by the **Pigeon River forestry field office** (off Sturgeon Valley Rd., 989/983-4101).

MAP SYMBOLS

▦	Expressway	**(**	Highlight	✗	Airfield	⚓	Golf Course
⋯	Primary Road	○	City/Town	✗	Airport	🅿	Parking Area
⋯	Secondary Road	◉	State Capital	▲	Mountain	⬟	Archaeological Site
⋯	Unpaved Road	⊛	National Capital	✛	Unique Natural Feature	⚑	Church
------	Trail	★	Point of Interest			🯄	Gas Station
⋯	Ferry	•	Accommodation	⋇	Waterfall	◠	Glacier
------	Railroad	▾	Restaurant/Bar	⚑	Park	▨	Mangrove
▦	Pedestrian Walkway	▪	Other Location	⬒	Trailhead	▨	Reef
⫴⫴⫴	Stairs	⋀	Campground	⤲	Skiing Area	▨	Swamp

CONVERSION TABLES

°C = (°F - 32) / 1.8
°F = (°C x 1.8) + 32
1 inch = 2.54 centimeters (cm)
1 foot = 0.304 meters (m)
1 yard = 0.914 meters
1 mile = 1.6093 kilometers (km)
1 km = 0.6214 miles
1 fathom = 1.8288 m
1 chain = 20.1168 m
1 furlong = 201.168 m
1 acre = 0.4047 hectares
1 sq km = 100 hectares
1 sq mile = 2.59 square km
1 ounce = 28.35 grams
1 pound = 0.4536 kilograms
1 short ton = 0.90718 metric ton
1 short ton = 2,000 pounds
1 long ton = 1.016 metric tons
1 long ton = 2,240 pounds
1 metric ton = 1,000 kilograms
1 quart = 0.94635 liters
1 US gallon = 3.7854 liters
1 Imperial gallon = 4.5459 liters
1 nautical mile = 1.852 km

°FAHRENHEIT °CELSIUS

°F	°C	
230	110	
220		
210	100	WATER BOILS
200	90	
190		
180	80	
170		
160	70	
150		
140	60	
130	50	
120		
110	40	
100		
90	30	
80		
70	20	
60		
50	10	
40		
30	0	WATER FREEZES
20	-10	
10		
0	-20	
-10		
-20	-30	
-30		
-40	-40	

INCH: 0 1 2 3 4

CM: 0 1 2 3 4 5 6 7 8 9 10

MOON MICHIGAN'S TRAVERSE BAYS
& MACKINAC ISLAND
Avalon Travel
a member of the Perseus Books Group
1700 Fourth Street
Berkeley, CA 94710, USA
www.moon.com

Editor: Erin Raber
Series Manager: Kathryn Ettinger
Copy Editor: Ann Seifert
Graphics Coordinator: Elizabeth Jang
Production Coordinator: Elizabeth Jang
Cover Designer: Kathryn Osgood
Map Editor: Kat Bennett
Cartographers: Kat Bennett, Stephanie Poulain

ISBN-13: 978-1-61238-789-5

KEEPING CURRENT

If you have a favorite gem you'd like to see included in the next edition, or see anything
that needs updating, clarification, or correction, please drop us a line. Send your com-
ments via email to feedback@moon.com, or use the address above.

ABOUT THE AUTHOR

Laura Martone

Laura Martone has been an avid traveler since childhood. While growing up, she and her mother would often take long road trips to fascinating U.S. landmarks, such as the Rocky Mountains and Monticello. After graduating from Northwestern University in 1998 with a dual degree in English and radio/TV/film, Laura continued to explore the United States with her husband, Daniel. Equally fond of cultural and natural wonders, she has a particular affinity for the state of Michigan, where she spends her summers.

Laura first traveled to the Great Lakes State in 2000 to visit her husband's family and has experienced a lot of this diverse locale ever since. She's searched for Petoskey stones along the shores of Lake Superior, picked wild blueberries in the woods of the Lower Peninsula, toured an active GM truck plant in the Flint area, explored the art galleries of Saugatuck and Douglas, and attended the National Cherry Festival in Traverse City – and she's not done yet.

When not in Michigan, Laura operates two film festivals with her husband and spends much of her time in New Orleans. She's contributed articles to *National Geographic Traveler, MotorHome, Route 66 Magazine, RV Journal,* and *The Ecotourism Observer.* In addition, she's written and edited several other guidebooks, including *Moon New Orleans, Moon Florida Keys, Moon Baja RV Camping,* and *Moon Metro Los Angeles.* For more about Laura's travels, visit her websites at www.wanderingsoles.com and www.americannomadtravel.com.

CPSIA information can be obtained at www.ICGtesting.com
Printed in the USA
LVOW12s0927100614

389391LV00006B/28/P